Genetic Genealogy
In Practice

National Genealogical Society
Special Topics Series

Genetic Genealogy In Practice

Blaine T. Bettinger
and
Debbie Parker Wayne

National Genealogical Society Special Topics Series
Genetic Genealogy In Practice

NGS Special Publications No. 120
ISBN No. 978-1-935815-22-8

Printed in the United States on chlorine-free, acid free, 30 percent post-consumer recycled paper.

Cover photos contributed by the authors.

Book Design: KarrieRoss.com

PUBLISHED BY
National Genealogical Society
3108 Columbia Pike, Suite 300
Arlington, VA 22204-4304

Acknowledgements and Dedication

This book was greatly improved by the generosity and contributions of others. We learned from discussions with colleagues at genetic genealogy and genealogy conferences and institutes. We are especially grateful to Patricia Lee Hobbs and Karen Stanbary for reviewing an early draft. We also offer thanks to the NGS Publications Committee, Genetic Genealogy Committee, and editor Laura Murphy DeGrazia for suggestions that helped simplify and clarify complex topics for the readers. Any errors remaining are our own.

Debbie Parker Wayne offers gratitude to all her family members who swabbed their cheeks or spit into a tube. I would like to thank co-author Blaine T. Bettinger for being so easy to work with and for inspiring me with his logical and rational thinking. I dedicate this book to my husband Jim who supports my genealogical endeavors, even when it means he stays home alone.

Blaine T. Bettinger thanks his family, friends, and colleagues for their support. This book would never have happened without Debbie's vision, and I can only hope that future colleagues are as wonderful to work with. I dedicate this book to my children Elijah and Logan, the best genetic genealogy project of all.

Contents

Preface

Genetic genealogy is the application of DNA evidence to genealogical research.

Since the launch of the first commercial genetic genealogy testing in 2000, millions of people across the world have purchased DNA tests to explore their ancestries. As a result, there is a continuing need for education and hands-on exercises that help genealogists understand the benefits and limitations of DNA testing. Genealogists will find hands-on exercises here, in the context of individual chapters that introduce different types of DNA testing and how testing can be used for genealogy.

This book focuses on the specifics of applying DNA test results and genetics as evidence to examine a genealogical question. Other excellent books are devoted to documentary research, analysis, and correlation, therefore this book will not empha-size those concepts. Every reader, however, should understand the importance of having a strong conclusion based on documentary evidence to correlate with DNA evidence. Both types of research—documentary and DNA—must meet genealogical standards if a resulting conclusion is to be considered credible.

The concepts and practical analysis data presented in this book should be applicable for quite some time. Transitory, step-by-step instructions on accessing DNA data or using specific tools are not included. Those processes change frequently; current information can easily be found online using a search engine or by reading blogs, mail lists, and forums identified in the "Reading and Source List" chapter. For example, *NGS Magazine,* published by the National Genealogical Society (NGS), offers a column by Debbie Parker Wayne. The October 2013 issue outlined steps to get started with genetic genealogy. Back issues of the magazine are available in the "Members Only" section of the NGS website (http://ngsgenealogy.org). Early articles are also available on Wayne's website (http://debbiewayne.com). Since March 2014, *APG Quarterly,* the journal of the Associ-ation of Professional Genealogists (APG), has published a column focusing on the needs of professional genetic genealogists. First written by Debbie Parker Wayne, and now by Blaine T. Bettinger, the articles are available in the "Members Only" section of the APG website (http://apgen.org).

Each chapter of this book introduces a type of DNA or a DNA-testing concept that is fundamental to the understanding and use of genetic genealogy. Chapters should be read in the order they are presented, and exercises at the end of each chapter should be attempted and mastered before moving on. This will help solidify the information presented and test the reader's understanding. Concepts in the final chapters require an understanding of multiple types of DNA testing. Jumping ahead without completely grasping all aspects of the four types of DNA—Y chromosome, mitochondrial, autoso-mal, and X chromosome—will make later chapters unnecessarily difficult.

For additional practice, examples in each chapter may be replaced with data from the reader's own research. The family trees in Appendix A, for example, can be replaced with those of other families. Colleagues and partners may exchange examples to check one another's work.

Genetic genealogy is a complex subject. It is challenging to grasp all the intricate details on the initial reading of a chapter. It may be necessary to read a chapter multiple times, with concepts becoming clearer upon each review.

An education in genetic genealogy will never be complete. Tests and tools are constantly being developed and changed. Newly discovered methodologies are being shared in forums, special interest groups, and mailing lists. After completing this book, interaction with other genetic genealogists will help readers stay on top of the latest developments.

CHAPTER 1

Basic Genetics

Genetic genealogy can be fully utilized and enjoyed without the need of an advanced degree in genetics or biology. Regardless of one's degree, experience, or background, working through this book will help the reader understand different types of DNA and their uses and limitations in genealogical research. Individual chapters of this book will cover specifics on the different types of DNA, but each chapter assumes an understanding of the basic genetic principles covered here.

Humans inherit several "types" of DNA, each of which can help genealogists research and confirm different portions of a family tree. Those types include

- mitochondrial DNA (mtDNA), found outside of the cell nucleus in tiny organelles called mitochondria (mitochondrion being the singular form);
- autosomal DNA (atDNA), which is composed of chromosomes 1–22 found in the cell nucleus; and
- the sex-determining chromosomes, Y-DNA and X-DNA, also found in the cell nucleus.

The twenty-two autosomes and the X and Y chromosomes collectively are called nuclear DNA, as they are contained within the nucleus. Figure 1 is a rudimentary diagram (not to scale) of a human cell, showing the nucleus and mitochondria.

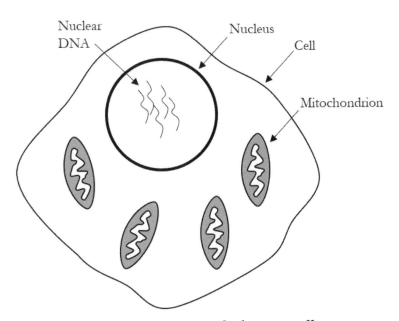

Figure 1. Diagram of a human cell

Prior to fertilization, a mother's egg contains the following DNA, which she passes down to her child:

- one copy of chromosomes 1–22 (the autosomes), represented in figure 2 as the numbers 1–22 in the inner circle or nucleus of the egg, some or all of which have recombined in a new way from the DNA inherited from both of the mother's parents
- an X chromosome, which potentially recombined in a new way from the DNA inherited from both of the mother's parents
- mtDNA inherited from the mother's mother, without recombination (represented by the small circles outside of the nucleus)

Prior to fertilization, a father's sperm contains the following DNA, which he passes down to his child:

- one copy of autosomes 1–22, represented in figure 2 as the numbers 1–22 in the oval, some or all of which have recombined in a new way from the DNA inherited from both of the father's parents
- either an X or a Y chromosome, neither of which has been recombined, the X coming from the father's mother, the Y coming from the father's father[1]

During fertilization, an egg cell containing DNA from the mother and a sperm cell containing DNA from the father combine to form a zygote. If the sperm that fertilizes the egg contains a Y chromosome, the resulting child will be male (with one X chromosome and one Y chromosome). If the sperm that fertilizes the egg contains an X chromosome, the resulting child will be female (with two X chromosomes, one from the father and one from the mother).

After fertilization, the chromosomes from the egg and sperm pair up inside the zygote to form twenty-three pairs of chromosomes. The mtDNA inherited from the mother will be contained outside the nucleus of the cell in the mitochondria.

Structure of the DNA Molecule

In humans, all DNA used for genetic genealogy has a primary structure and a secondary structure.[2] These structures are analogous to a book, with the primary structure being words and the secondary structure being paragraphs. Similarities in two books would be discovered by comparing the words—the primary structure.

The "paragraphs" of the DNA molecule are the winding, double-helix structures of the chromosome. The "words" of the DNA molecule are the base pairs of that chromosome. If a chromosome or molecule was completely unwound and was large enough to see with the naked eye, it would resemble a ladder. Figure 3 illustrates a DNA ladder.

---

[1] Although the tips of the Y chromosome, called the pseudo-autosomal region, do potentially recombine with the X chromosome, the majority of the Y chromosome (including every region used for genetic genealogy analysis) is passed on to the next generation intact. This limited recombination between the X and Y chromosome can therefore be ignored.

[2] There are actually higher levels of structure, but they are not currently used in genetic genealogy. Recent studies suggest this structure may be inheritable for at least several generations. If so, those higher levels of structure could ultimately be used for genetic genealogy purposes.

For each DNA chromosome or molecule, the rungs of the ladder are numbered beginning with one at the first rung. Each rung consists of two adjoining sides. Each side is formed by one of four chemicals: guanine, cytosine, adenine, and thymine. Each chemical, or nucleotide, is commonly referred to using the first letter of its name (G, C, A, or T). Each chemical base can only pair with one other to form the rungs of the ladder: guanine pairs with cytosine, and adenine pairs with thymine. This is also visible in figure 3.

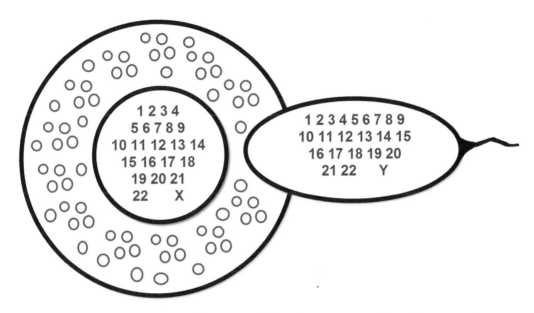

Figure 2. Fertilization of the egg cell by the sperm cell to form a zygote with mitochondrial DNA and twenty-three pairs of chromosomes

Each rung of the ladder—a single location on the chromosome or the mtDNA molecule—contains a nucleotide base pair. In genetic genealogy, a variation at one location (or base pair) of the multi-rung ladder is called a single nucleotide polymorphism (SNP). A second type of variation is a short tandem repeat (STR), in which a sequence of bases, for example "GATA," is repeated a certain number of times. SNP and STR locations may be referred to as "markers" and can have marker names. The value of a SNP marker is the chemical base at that position (G, C, A, or T, also called the allele); the value of an STR marker is the number of times the sequence repeats (which is 3 in the example shown in figure 3).

Almost all—99.9 percent—of the DNA of any two people on earth is exactly the same. Accordingly, genetic genealogy tests are only interested in the 0.1 percent of DNA that can vary from one person to the next. Those differences help genetic genealogists determine kinship. When these variable DNA markers or locations are compared between two people, matches and mismatches are identified. The more matches and fewer mismatches, the more closely related are those two people.[3] Identical twins will have almost

---

[3] Joel T. Dudley and Konrad J. Karczewski, *Exploring Personal Genomics* (Oxford, UK: Oxford University Press, 2013), 16.

no mismatches, while fifth cousins will share only a few segments of DNA and thus will not match across the vast majority of the tested regions.

Currently genetic genealogists can order three kinds of DNA tests—mitochondrial DNA, Y chromosome DNA, and autosomal DNA—which examine a total of four DNA types (the X chromosome being tested along with the autosomes).

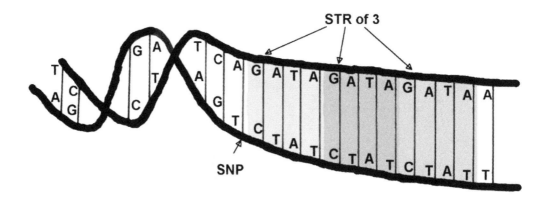

Figure 3. The DNA helix indicating SNP and STR markers

Y Chromosome DNA (Y-DNA)
The Y chromosome is one of the two sex chromosomes (the other being the X chromosome), both of which are located within the nucleus of the cell. Only males have a Y chromosome, which is fifty-eight million base pairs long. It contains approximately two hundred genes involved in sperm production and a wide variety of cellular functions.

The Y chromosome is passed down from a father only to his sons. Y-DNA tests are useful for examining ancient origins of a test-taker's paternal line and for finding close paternal relatives in a testing database. Y-DNA tests analyze either SNPs or STRs. SNP tests are used to learn about ancient ancestry, while STR tests (which typically examine 37, 67, or 111 STR markers) are useful for exploring recent genealogical relationships.

Y-DNA is covered in detail in chapter 3.

Mitochondrial DNA (mtDNA)
Mitochondrial DNA is a single circular piece of DNA found within a cell's mitochondria. A cell can have hundreds of mitochondria, and each mitochondrion can have more than one copy of DNA. The mtDNA is approximately 16,569 base pairs long; the exact length varies depending on whether mutations have resulted in additions or deletions of base pairs. The mtDNA encodes thirty-seven genes that support the mitochondria's role as a cell's energy factory.

Only a mother passes down mitochondrial DNA to her children. A male inherits his mother's mtDNA but does not pass it down to the next generation. This type of DNA test is useful for investigating ancient origins of a test-taker's maternal line and for identifying relatively close maternal relatives in a testing database. Early mtDNA tests sequenced (that is, determined the exact base pair order) a very small portion of mtDNA. More recent tests sequence the entire 16,569 base pairs. It is also possible to analyze ancient origins of mtDNA by testing SNPs located along the mitochondrial DNA.

Mitochondrial DNA is covered in detail in chapter 4.

Autosomal DNA (atDNA)

Autosomal DNA comprises the twenty-two pairs of chromosomes (called autosomes) found within the nucleus of the cell. One of each pair of the chromosomes comes from the subject's mother, while the other copy comes from the subject's father. Before being passed down to the next generation, atDNA undergoes recombination, a process by which the two copies of the chromosomes optionally exchange one or more pieces of DNA. Consequently, one of the biggest challenges of using atDNA in genealogy is determining the origin of inherited segments.

Autosomal DNA tests can either sequence every base pair along the DNA ladder or detect targeted SNPs. Currently only SNP tests are used by the major companies, with tests looking at hundreds of thousands of SNPs along all twenty-three chromosome pairs (that is, the autosomes and the sex chromosomes). In the future, as the price of sequencing declines, whole-genome sequencing may be offered.

Results of atDNA testing are used to estimate ethnicity and to identify segments of DNA shared by two or more individuals. The amount of DNA shared by two people can be used to hypothesize their genealogical relationship, particularly if the relationship is recent. Relationship predictions based on shared DNA generally assume only one common ancestral link between the test-takers. In the real world, however, many people share more than one recent ancestral link. This possibility must be factored into every DNA analysis. Additionally, random mutations and recombination cause some relatives to share more or less DNA than expected. Relationship predictions cannot be precise unless they involve very close relationships (usually at the level of second cousin or closer). There are few hard-and-fast rules when using atDNA comparisons to determine how two people are related.

Autosomal DNA is covered in detail in chapter 5.

X Chromosome DNA (X-DNA)

The X chromosome is one of the two sex chromosomes (the other being the Y chromosome), both of which are located within the nucleus of the cell. A male has one X chromosome, which he receives from his mother. A female has two X chromosomes, one of which she receives from her father and the other from her mother. The X chromosome is approximately 156 million base pairs long and contains approximately two thousand genes involved in many different cellular functions.

X-chromosome testing is used primarily for ethnicity estimates and for matching with other test-takers. Because of the chromosome's unique inheritance pattern, X-DNA matching can be narrowed to significantly fewer lines than atDNA. Some genetic genealogists believe that a significant number of X-DNA matches are false positives due to the low SNP density of current testing and the very low matching-thresholds set by the testing companies. Case studies incorporating X-DNA and atDNA should provide clarity as to the true number of false positive and false negative matches on X-DNA and atDNA segments.

The X chromosome is covered in detail in chapter 6.

DNA Match

The term "DNA match" is used throughout this book in two ways, depending on context. In some places, DNA match refers to a person who is on the list of those who have segments or markers that match a test-taker. In other places, the term is used generically to indicate a match on the tested DNA segments of the people under discussion. The meaning should be clear from the context.

Genetic Distance

Genetic distance indicates how closely two test-takers match one another. It is measured differently for different types of DNA tests. A smaller genetic distance usually, but not always, indicates fewer generations back to a common ancestor, referred to as the Most Recent Common Ancestor (MRCA).

For Y-DNA STR tests and mtDNA tests, genetic distance is a calculation of the number of markers that differ between the test-takers' results. Fewer differences indicate a closer relationship is likely. For atDNA and X-DNA tests, genetic distance is based on the number and length of shared DNA- segments. More and longer shared segments usually indicate a closer relationship. There are, however, other factors to be considered, as discussed in later chapters.

Haplogroups

A haplogroup is a name given to a large branch of the human genetic tree. There are two separate human haplogroup trees, one for Y-DNA and one for mtDNA. Both have many branches. A haplogroup assignment indicates to which branch of the tree a test-taker belongs. Some haplogroup assignments place a person only on a main branch of the tree. A person can later be assigned to a sub-branch either because of a better understanding of the tree or as a result of more in-depth testing.

The first letter of the haplogroup designates the main branch of the tree to which a test-taker belongs. Subsequent letters and numbers provide a more defined haplogroup and place a test-taker on a sub-branch or sub-clade of the main haplogroup or clade.

Haplogroup assignments indicate whether two test-takers have a common ancestor who lived thousands or tens of thousands of years ago. Haplogroups also can indicate whether two people are recently related. Two test-takers in different mtDNA haplogroups do not share a common ancestor in the matrilineal line within a genealogical timeframe. Similarly, two test-takers in different Y-DNA haplogroups do not share a common ancestor in the patrilineal line within a genealogical timeframe. Again, there are other factors to be considered, as discussed in later chapters.

CHAPTER 2

Genetic Genealogy, Standards, And Ethics

DNA evidence can be used to support or reject a genealogical hypothesis, just like a census record, a birth certificate, or a deed. As with any traditional documentary source, DNA evidence is never used on its own; instead, it is evaluated, analyzed, and correlated with multiple pieces of evidence.

The proper use of DNA evidence to support a genealogical conclusion must allow those who did not directly perform the research—that is, those who did not see the DNA test results—to evaluate the strength of the conclusion without having to repeat the research. One of the most widely used measures to evaluate a genealogical conclusion is the Genealogical Proof Standard (GPS), published by the Board for Certification of Genealogists (BCG). Although it is not the only standard available, the five criteria of the GPS lend themselves exceptionally well to solutions incorporating DNA evidence. Other standards employ different terminology, but ultimately all require similar evidence analysis.

What is the GPS?

The GPS is a set of criteria used to evaluate the credibility of a genealogical conclusion. A description of the elements of the GPS and explanations of the use of those elements are available online.[1] *Genealogy Standards*[2] and *Mastering Genealogical Proof*[3] include more detailed explanations. Readers who are not yet familiar with the GPS may wish to study these references before moving on.

This chapter covers criteria specific to the use of DNA evidence in the context of a genealogical question and how to determine the extent of DNA evidence required to form or support a credible conclusion.

Table 1 explains how information in this book helps researchers incorporate DNA evidence in a conclusion that can meet the GPS.

---

[1] "Certification: Frequently Asked Questions," Question 9, *Board for Certification of Genealogists* (http://www.bcgcertification.org/certification/faq.html#9). "The Genealogical Proof Standard," *Board for Certification of Genealogists* (http://www.bcgcertification.org/resources/standard.html).
[2] Board for Certification of Genealogists, *Genealogy Standards*, 50th anniversary ed. (Nashville, TN: Ancestry Imprint, Turner Publishing, 2014), 1–3.
[3] Thomas W. Jones, *Mastering Genealogical Proof* (Arlington, VA: National Genealogical Society, 2013).

Table 1. The five elements of the GPS and how this book addresses them

GPS element	How this book addresses the GPS element
reasonably exhaustive research	Helps researchers determine the type and extent of DNA evidence needed
complete and accurate source citations	Discusses citations in the chapter titled "Incorporating DNA Evidence in a Written Conclusion"
analysis and correlation of all evidence	Helps researchers analyze the DNA evidence and correlate it accurately with other evidence
resolution of conflicting evidence	Helps researcher understand and discuss evidence conflicts
soundly reasoned, coherently written conclusion	Helps researchers reason about and logically organize DNA evidence; provides writing tips in the chapter titled "Incorporating DNA Evidence in a Written Conclusion"

How Genetic Genealogy Relates to the GPS

The first element of the GPS calls for thorough research: "*Reasonably exhaustive research* ensures examination of all potentially relevant sources. It minimizes the risk that undiscovered evidence will overturn a too-hasty conclusion."[4] Clearly, genetic genealogy has matured to the point where DNA evidence is a potentially relevant source to examine many questions, and thus DNA testing should be considered whenever it can be considered.

Determining whether DNA evidence should be considered, and whether it can be obtained, is a multi-step process. The genealogist must first determine whether DNA evidence is applicable to the genealogical question. Is the answer to the question something that could potentially be supported or rejected using DNA evidence? If not, DNA tests are not necessary. If so, ignoring the use of DNA evidence could result in an incorrect conclusion.

Many factors contribute to how critical DNA evidence may be. For example, when there are several men with the same name in a location at the same time, DNA may help the researcher be sure the correct man is included in the family tree. Limitations of DNA evidence may sometimes mean that it cannot conclusively confirm a hypothesis—but using DNA evidence can sometimes conclusively refute proposed kinship or can provide supporting evidence for a genealogical conclusion.

After determining that DNA evidence may be applicable to the problem, the genealogist must identify the appropriate DNA test(s) and find a proper—and willing—test-taker. It is not enough that a question could potentially be analyzed with DNA evidence. The genealogist must find one or more living people who (1) descend from the person on whom the research is focused; (2) inherited the type of DNA necessary to analyze the question—atDNA, Y-DNA, X-DNA, mtDNA; and (3) are willing to take a DNA test.

---

[4] Board for Certification of Genealogists, *Genealogy Standards*, 2.

Knowing who to test and what test to use is complicated due to the fact that each type of DNA follows a different inheritance path. Some types of DNA randomly recombine, while others do not. DNA copying errors (mutations) occur at random times in random locations. These factors, which are discussed in detail in later chapters, must be considered when deciding which DNA test or tests a given person should take.

Advantages to Using DNA

When used in genealogical research, DNA offers several advantages over documentary evidence. Documents may contain untruths. These could arise because an informant lied or did not have the correct information, because a scribe misheard the information or erroneously recorded it, because a transcriber erred, or because of some other error or intentional act. In contrast, as long as DNA evidence is correctly interpreted, it does not contain untruths.

Among the main advantages of using DNA evidence are that DNA can
- corroborate documentary research;
- provide clues to guide documentary research; and
- supply evidence where no known documents exist.

Types of Genealogical Problems for Which DNA Can Provide Applicable Evidence

Just like other record types, DNA evidence is not useful in solving every genealogical problem. The types of genealogical questions for which it can provide evidence are described in detail in later chapters. In general, however, DNA may provide evidence to determine whether
- test-takers share a common ancestor, recently or in the distant past;
- a uniparental line (Y-DNA or mtDNA) traces back to a specific biogeographical population (such as African or Native American); or
- test-takers may have a recent ancestor from a specific biogeographical population.

DNA evidence is useful in locating potential biological relations for adoptees, and it is frequently used to corroborate a hypothesis where documentary research alone has not provided a clear answer. By itself DNA evidence can give a clear indication of a parent-child or sibling relationship. For all other relationships, DNA evidence must be correlated with documentary evidence to reach a credible conclusion.

How Much DNA Evidence is Needed?

After a genealogist determines that a particular type of DNA test may provide evidence to help resolve a question and that at least one living descendant is willing to participate, the genealogist must determine (1) the DNA-test resolution (that is, the number of DNA locations or markers tested) that will provide the strongest evidence; and (2) the number of people who should be tested. With a few rare exceptions (such as ethnicity or ancient-ancestry analysis), genetic genealogy provides answers by comparing DNA test results of a test-taker to one or more other people in a database (belonging either to a testing company or a third party). Often, more than one test-taker is needed to obtain a meaningful amount of evidence; sometimes many test-takers are required. Multiple test-takers may be identified and recruited by a genealogist, but in some cases reasonably close relatives have already tested and their results are already in an existing database.

There are no hard-and-fast answers as to the number of test-takers needed. The recommended number of test-takers varies based on factors such as the number of potential test-takers available, distance to the test-takers' common ancestor, DNA mutations that may have occurred in the line to the test-takers, and inheritance patterns and recombination aspects of the type of DNA being tested. It sometimes is economical to begin with a small number of test-takers and decide on additional testing based on the early results. In other scenarios there may only be a single living person capable or willing to take the required DNA test, in which case the genealogist will only have that DNA evidence with which to work. In still other cases no suitable tester will be available.

As an example, consider a problem in which a genealogist seeks to determine if nine different Y-DNA lines link back to the same male ancestor born about 1700. A minimum of nine test-takers would be needed—one in each of the lines being studied. It is highly likely, depending on the number of men who had sons in each line in each generation, that dozens of men would have to be tested to reach a credible conclusion. Even then, the available Y-DNA evidence might not be able to answer the question definitively. Regardless, the starting point for determining how many test-takers are needed, and for determining the best individuals to test, is always an accurate family tree that is as complete as possible.

Importance of Tree Accuracy and Depth

The accuracy and completeness of family trees belonging to a test-taker and that test-taker's DNA matches greatly impact a genealogist's ability to analyze and correlate DNA information. An inaccurate tree may make finding a common ancestor impossible. An incomplete tree may make locating a common ancestor difficult because that ancestor may not yet be known. An incomplete tree might also mislead a genealogist to assume that shared DNA comes from a known common ancestor when some of the matching DNA could have come from a yet-unidentified common ancestor.

An individual's genetic tree and genealogical tree are not duplicates. A genealogical tree includes all of a person's ancestors at every generation, even if some may not yet be identified. An individual's genetic tree includes only those ancestors who contributed to that person's DNA. Due to random recombination and inheritance patterns of DNA, some ancestors in a genealogical tree will not have provided an individual with any DNA—or the amount inherited is too small to be detected and effectively utilized. Because the genetic family tree includes only some of a person's ancestors, a test-taker will not be able to find DNA evidence to answer every question. For example, there could have been a Native American eighth great-grandmother in the family tree, but when random recombination and inheritance result in little or none of her atDNA being passed down to the test-taker, an atDNA test will not show any Native American ancestry. In this case, the absence of DNA evidence is not proof of the absence of Native American ancestry; the DNA testing provides no evidence to help answer the question either way.

Some researchers are only interested in documenting biological relationships, while others include biological, adoptive, step, and fictive kin. Biological kin are those with a biological relationship, what has traditionally been called "blood kin." Adoptive relatives have no biological relationship or perhaps a different biological relationship than the one indicated by their place in the family structure. Adoption may be documented or undocumented. It may be known to all members of the family or to only a few. Step relationships are formed due to multiple marriages or relationships, such as the joining of two people with children from prior relationships. Fictive kin are those we refer to as family members although there is no biological or legal relationship. For example, many people refer to a parent's close friend as an aunt, uncle, or cousin. Inclusion of non-biological relationships in a family tree can cause confusion in the search for a common ancestor. Although non-biological relationships are just as important and valid to our lives and to human history as biological relationships—in many cases even more so—they are impossible to examine with genetic genealogy testing. Genetic genealogy is inherently focused on biological relationships, which is an important limitation to keep in mind.

Family trees of future generations may be subject to even more questions. For decades children have been conceived from sperm and egg donors, through surrogate parents, and with other assisted-reproduction methods. Those methods yield children with two biological parents, regardless of the number or gender of parents raising the child. Today, however, technology is beginning to replace segments of DNA in embryos. For example, current technology allows mtDNA to be replaced in eggs or embryos where a mother's own mtDNA is unhealthy.[5] The technology to splice genes into our chromosomes also exists.[6] In the future some children may have three or more biological parents.

Unexpected Findings Resulting from DNA Testing

All genealogical sources, including DNA, have the potential to reveal unexpected relationships or the lack of an expected relationship. Genetic genealogists must anticipate these possibilities and consider the potential emotions and reactions of all involved. Whether something is learned from a document or from DNA evidence, ethics guide what should be revealed, to whom it should be revealed, and how it should be revealed. When asking someone to take a DNA test, it is important to make the person aware of the possibilities.

---

[5] Gretchen Vogel, "U.K. Agency Cautiously Endorses Mitochondria Replacement," ScienceInsider, News, *Science*, 20 March 2013 (http://news.sciencemag.org/health/2013/03/u.k.-agency-cautiously-endorses-mitochondria-replacement).

[6] Nicole Giese, "Technique Enables Efficient Gene Splicing in Human Embryonic Stem Cells," Whitehead Institute for Biomedical Research; reprint, *Science Daily*, 14 August 2009 (http://www.sciencedaily.com/releases/2009/08/090813142146.htm).

An individual's reaction to unexpected findings can range from none to minimal to major, depending on how far back the event happened and the degree of personal investment in the test results. For example, a DNA test may reveal that the documented father of a focus person is not the biological father. If the tested person is a fourth great-grandchild of the focus person, the result may not seem important to the test-taker. If, however, the focus person is the test-taker, the result could cause significant difficulties between living persons. If the focus person is famous or a favorite person of any family member, there may be reluctance to accept the evidence provided by the DNA test results. DNA evidence that shows no biological relationship between members of the family tree can cause stress and resistance in the family historian who has invested countless hours in researching the family.

Ethically, it is important to discuss possible outcomes with a DNA test-taker before the test is taken. Asking whether the test-taker wants to know the results, whatever the findings, can alleviate some problems, although it cannot completely prevent the potential emotional impact of an unexpected test result. Dealing with unexpected results of DNA testing may require careful consideration, diplomacy, and tact until those most affected are no longer living. Genetic genealogists should present the facts in an unemotional and unbiased way that is respectful of the feelings of the test-taker.

Genetic Genealogy Standards and Ethical Issues

Standards for the evaluation of traditional genealogical research have been available for decades. The current revision, *Genealogy Standards,*[7] discusses the need to use DNA evidence, but does not go into specifics on how to incorporate it.

In 2013 a group of genetic genealogists formed an ad hoc committee to define standards for incorporating genetic genealogy into genealogical research. The resulting Genetic Genealogy Standards were published in January 2015.[8] The Genetic Genealogy Standards, which complement *Genealogy Standards*, are for every genealogist who uses DNA evidence in their work—not just for professional genealogists or experienced genetic genealogists. See chapter 8 for more on the standards.

A major area of emphasis in the standards is the recognition that every person has a right to consent to or refuse DNA testing. Test-takers should understand how the testing company will use the DNA data and what information may be available to other parties. They should understand that any information available online could be accessed by third parties—who may use the data without permission. The standards make no judgment as to whether these things are good or bad, just that the test-taker should understand them in order to make an educated decision. In the same way that some genealogists post their entire family trees online and some do not, some test-takers find it perfectly acceptable to have their entire genome sequenced and publicly available, while others may be more reticent.

---

[7] Board for Certification of Genealogists, *Genealogy Standards.*
[8] *Genetic Genealogy Standards* (http://www.geneticgenealogystandards.com).

Standards guiding several subjects are still in progress. These include recommendations for minimum testing in various situations, interpretation of results, and citation elements. Items will be added when available and the standards will be updated periodically as advancements are made in analysis techniques and testing procedures.

Genealogical testing focuses on the use of DNA markers as evidence in kinship, identity, and ancestry, but some medically significant markers are also tested. Some companies focus on health research, with genetic genealogy considered a secondary market. Given the potential medical implications and privacy concerns, the best practices in the Genetic Genealogy Standards balance genealogical use with privacy. If all genealogists follow the standards the chance of conflict between researchers and test-takers will be significantly reduced.

Considerations When Asking a Person to Participate in a DNA Study for Genealogical Purposes

Genealogists should only obtain DNA for testing with the consent of the test-taker. To make an informed decision about consent, a prospective test-taker should be intellectually capable and have the legal right to make the decision. The test-taker should understand the possible outcomes and reports, as well as what will be done with the DNA sample and the test results:

- Effective use of test results for genealogy requires sharing some DNA information and some family tree information. Some test results have medical implications.
- Any DNA results shared on a public web page may be copied and used by other parties.
- DNA tests, as well as other genealogical sources, can reveal unexpected information.
- A company's Terms of Service and Consent Agreements determine what may be done with the DNA data. Some companies only run tests and provide data to the test-taker. Some use the DNA data for other purposes, by de-identifying and aggregating the data of all test-takers. Some companies allow a person to opt out of these uses, but some do not.
- Some companies test in the country in which a DNA sample originates. Some companies send samples to other countries for testing.

The test-taker must decide how much information will be shared, and whether to reveal his or her real name. Complete anonymity can never be guaranteed in the age of the Internet, even with the level of security available today. The test-taker should specify whether a real name or a pseudonym should be used when DNA data is published or shared.

International and Jurisdictional Considerations

Each country, state, or province may have different laws on the use of DNA. Before ordering or mailing DNA test kits, genealogists must understand the laws of their own country as well as those for the country or countries in which the test-takers live. The Genetic Information Nondiscrimination Act (GINA) was passed in the United States in 2008:

> The law protects people from discrimination by health insurers and employers on the basis of DNA information. The law does not cover life insurance, disability insurance and long-term care insurance. Before the federal law was passed, many states had passed laws against genetic discrimination. The degree of protection from these laws varies widely among the different states. The federal law sets a minimum standard of protection that must be met in all states. It does not weaken the protections provided by any state law.[9]

GINA, however, does not provide absolute protection. It does not apply to long-term-care- or life-insurers, and it does not apply to businesses with fewer than fifteen employees. Further, as with all laws, some people willfully violate it and some may violate it due to misunderstanding. Any person who believes he or she has been discriminated against due to genetic information should consult a lawyer.

International laws include the European Union's Data Protection Directive (now evolving into the General Data Protection Regulation)[10] and the United Kingdom's Data Protection Act,[11] among others.

CONCLUSIONS

DNA evidence alone seldom provides an answer to a genealogical question. Instead, the DNA evidence must be analyzed and correlated with a collection of other evidence. The strength of any conclusion resulting from the correlation and assembly of DNA and other evidence can be evaluated utilizing the GPS.

When using any genealogical source, including DNA, numerous factors specific to each source must be considered. For DNA, those factors include whether such evidence could shed light on the given question and whether DNA evidence is available and may be obtained. When incorporating DNA testing in research, genealogists must consider the associated ethical issues as well as the potential emotional impact that DNA test results may have on test-takers and their families.

---

[9] "Genetic Information Nondiscrimination Act of 2008," National Institutes of Health, *National Human Genome Research Institute* (https://www.genome.gov/10002328).

[10] "Data Protection Directive," *Wikipedia* (http://en.wikipedia.org/wiki/Data_Protection_Directive).

[11] "Data Protection," United Kingdom, *Your Rights and the Law* (https://www.gov.uk/data-protection/the-data-protection-act).

Chapter 2 Exercises

1. The goal is to determine when Isaac Ryan first bought land in what is now Jackson County, Mississippi. Can DNA evidence help achieve this goal? If so, how?

   _____

   _____

   _____

2. The goal is to determine whether the Isaac Ryan who first bought land in 1798 in what is now Jackson County, Mississippi, is the ancestor of Jonathan Ryan. Can DNA evidence help achieve this goal? If so, how?

   _____

   _____

   _____

3. Nathan suspects that Ethan Kilgore disinherited his sons Hugh and Philip just before his death in 1861 because, according to family legend, Ethan's wife informed him in a fit of rage that they weren't actually his children. Instead, the legend goes, they were the children of a former neighbor called Simon or Samuel Smith. Research in census records reveals a Samuel Simons living next door in 1820 and 1830, years that bookend the decade during which Hugh and Philip were born. Can DNA evidence be utilized to examine the question of why Ethan Kilgore disinherited his sons?

   _____

   _____

   _____

Henry is a professional genealogist and has been hired by Charles DuMond to research his DuMond line. Charles suspects his grandfather William DuMond was born William Rivers, but he has been unable to prove the name change. Charles has asked Henry to find evidence to support or refute the Rivers surname hypothesis. Using this scenario, answer questions 4 and 5.

4. Henry has been a professional genealogist for twenty-five years and is well versed in every record type that could be utilized for this project. However Henry is skeptical of DNA testing, and has never used or explored it in his or his clients' research.

Can Henry's research satisfy the GPS for this project if he intentionally doesn't consider DNA because he doesn't believe it is accurate?

_____

_____

_____

5. Henry decides to inform his client that Y-DNA or atDNA testing could potentially shed light on the question, but that he is not educated on the subject. Henry suggests that he or the client contact another genealogist who is well versed in the use of DNA. The client informs Henry that he isn't interested in that option. Can Henry complete the assigned project with any confidence, and can the project satisfy the GPS?

_____

_____

_____

Genealogist Julianna Turner has researched the Wilcox family in and around Jonesborough, Tennessee, for the past two decades. Based on the documentary evidence, she hypothesizes that Benjamin Wilcox is the father of the three males responsible for the three main Wilcox families in the region. Julianna would like to conduct Y-DNA testing on the three Wilcox lines to support or reject her hypothesis. Although there is the possibility that atDNA might shed light on the question, at the time being she is only considering Y-DNA. Using this scenario, answer questions 6 and 7.

6. After extensive research Julianna discovers that the first Wilcox family, descended from Thomas Wilcox, has thousands of descendants but no direct-line male descendants. If Y-DNA testing of the Thomas Wilcox line is impossible, and atDNA testing is not possible for various other reasons, can Julianna's research satisfy the GPS when analyzing whether Thomas Wilcox was the son of Benjamin Wilcox?

_____

_____

_____

7. Some years later, Julianna learns that before he died the last man with Thomas Wilcox's Y-DNA had a son that the family didn't know about. This living son is in fact the last-known male with Thomas Wilcox's Y-DNA. When Julianna contacts him, he refuses to undergo any type of DNA testing. If DNA testing of the Thomas Wilcox line is possible but cannot be performed due to refusal by the last living direct-line male, can Julianna's research satisfy the GPS when analyzing whether Thomas Wilcox was the son of Benjamin Wilcox?

_____

_____

_____

8. Brenda is working on a Kinship Determination Project (KDP) for submission in her BCG application portfolio. A KDP is a narrative genealogy, lineage, or pedigree that documents at least three ancestral generations. Like other genealogical proofs, a KDP requires that "the underlying research [is] reasonably thorough" and that Brenda consult "all sources and information items that competent genealogists would use to support the conclusion."[12] Brenda's KDP is based on her paternal grandfather's family. Her research has revealed that her great-grandfather Ronald was the product of a widely known but mostly undocumented non-paternal event; all the available evidence points to a single man as the biological father. Her own atDNA testing has proven largely inconclusive, despite testing herself and numerous third and fourth cousins. Y-DNA testing may be the final piece of evidence needed to confidently conclude the identity of Ronald's father. Brenda's father—Ronald's grandson—is still living and is the last person available for the Y-DNA test. He has advanced Alzheimer's disease and doesn't recognize Brenda. Although Brenda's father's legal representative has signed off on the DNA tests without reservation, Brenda has decided that it would be unethical to test her father. Instead she submits the KDP without any Y-DNA evidence, even though it is technically available to her. Can her KDP satisfy the GPS, or has she failed to conduct thorough research that considers all sources?

_____

_____

_____

9. Sadly, Brenda's father passes away before she submits her KDP. The Genetic Genealogy Standards provide that "in the case of a deceased individual, consent can be obtained from a legal representative."[13] The legal representative authorizes a Y-DNA test at the request of Brenda's sister, Rachel. Rachel receives the results and offers to share them with Brenda. However, Brenda has reservations about using the results without her father's explicit authorization, and submits her KDP without any Y-DNA evidence. Can her KDP satisfy the GPS, or has she failed to conduct thorough research that considers all sources?

_____

_____

_____

---

[12] Board for Certification of Genealogists, _Genealogy Standards_, 31 (Standard 51).
[13] _Genetic Genealogy Standards,_ Standard 2.

CHAPTER 3

Genealogical Applications for Y-DNA

What is Y-DNA?

One of the oldest and most powerful genetic genealogy tools is the Y chromosome. Y-DNA testing offers numerous benefits to genetic genealogists, due in large part to its inheritance pattern and lack of significant recombination. Because each man's Y chromosome is nearly identical to the Y chromosome that his many-great-grandfather possessed, the Y-DNA line can be traced back very far—on the order of thousands of years.

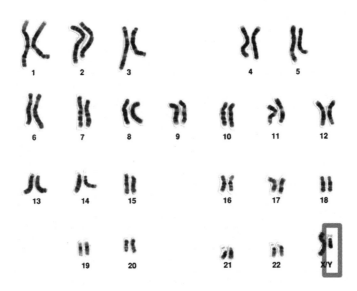

Figure 1. Human karyotype (National Human Genome Research Institute)

The human Y chromosome is one of the smallest chromosomes, with approximately fifty-seven million base pairs and just over two hundred genes. It is one of the two sex chromosomes, the other being the X chromosome.

Unlike all other chromosomes, the Y chromosome does not undergo extensive recombination before it is passed down to the next generation. There can be some recombination between the very tips of the Y and X chromosomes, but those regions are not used for genetic genealogy.

Y-DNA Inheritance Pattern

The path through which Y-DNA is passed is often referred to as a person's patrilineal line. See the pedigree chart in figure 2, on which the patrilineal line is shaded.

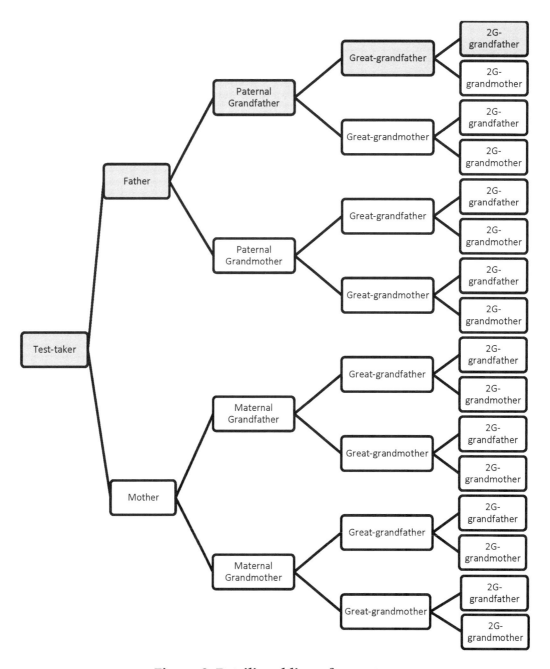

Figure 2. Patrilineal line of ancestors

In figure 3, the Y-DNA inheritance is shown in a descendancy chart. Circles represent women and squares represent men. The top row represents a couple. Children of the couple, two sons and one daughter, are shown on the second row, along with their mates. Grandchildren and their mates are shown on the third row. Great-grandchildren are shown on the fourth row. A male passes his Y-DNA only to his male children. Because of this inheritance pattern, only the males with a "y" in the square will have the Y-DNA passed down from the man in the top row. If only those on the bottom row are still living, there are only two potential Y-DNA test-takers in this family for any question related to the Y-DNA of the man at the top. In many cultures, the surname follows the patrilineal line, meaning there is a strong connection between the Y chromosome and the surname.

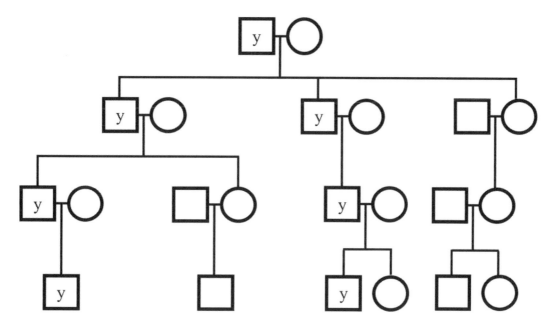

Figure 3. Patrilineal line of descendants

Advantages and Limitations of Y-DNA

The unique inheritance pattern of Y-DNA offers both advantages and limitations when applying test results to a genealogical problem. The lack of recombination means that the same Y-DNA footprint is passed down for many generations, allowing a line to be traced many generations back in time. Due to the relatively high rate of Y-DNA mutations, it is often possible to roughly estimate how much time has passed since two men had a common ancestor in their patrilineal line. Significant mismatch of two Y-DNA test-takers can definitively rule out a relationship on the patrilineal line.

The fact that the same Y-DNA footprint is passed down for many generations is a major advantage when trying to determine if a patrilineal line was of a specific biogeographical origin, such as African or Native American.[1] The origin-identifying markers will not be diluted by recombination and will persist through all generations.

---

[1] While Y-DNA can indicate Native American ancestry on the patrilineal line, it usually cannot determine which tribe a person may have been part of.

The same characteristics that make Y-DNA so useful also create limitations. It is impossible to determine, for example, which of a man's sons or grandsons is the ancestor of a particular line. An exact Y-DNA match can provide evidence that is consistent with a common ancestor, while not proving which man in that patrilineal line is that ancestor.

Test Strategies for Y-DNA

Genealogical questions that Y-DNA may be able to help answer include (1) whether a patrilineal line descends from a specific biogeographical origin, such as African or Native American; (2) whether it is possible that two men were in the same patrilineal line; and (3) from which of two men a person descends, assuming those two men are not related through their patrilineal lines.

After it is determined that Y-DNA may help answer a question, it is necessary to determine if there are living descendants who can take the test. Descendant family trees will be needed to trace a patrilineal line. A speculative tree, drawn by hand or created in a software program, can be created to track known descendants of the focus man. Starting with that ancestor, each descendant who inherited his Y-DNA should be marked, as illustrated in figure 3. The marked living descendants can be asked to take the Y-DNA test. If there are no living descendants in the patrilineal line, or if a living descendant is not willing to test, it may be necessary to research back a generation to see if the focus Y-DNA ancestor had brothers who may have living descendants in the patrilineal line. If a test candidate is still not found, it may be necessary to research back another generation to see if the focus Y-DNA ancestor had paternal uncles who may have living descendants in the patrilineal line. Because Y-DNA is passed down without recombination, it is possible to research back many generations in the search for potential Y-DNA test-takers.

If potential test-takers can be identified, the required test resolution must be determined.

Types of Y-DNA Testing

There are two main types of Y-DNA testing for genetic genealogy: Short Tandem Repeat (STR) and Single Nucleotide Polymorphism (SNP). The tests look at different kinds of markers, provide different information, and have different uses and limitations. Results of both test types are compared to the results of other test-takers in the company's database or in a DNA project or both. Projects may be established for test-takers sharing a surname, a common ancestor, a haplogroup, ancestry from a geographic region, and other shared interests.

1. Y-DNA STRs

STR markers are very short regions located along the Y chromosome. Each is made up of multiple copies of a short sequence of nucleotide bases that repeat a variable number of times. Each STR marker has a unique name. Most begin with the letters DYS (D=DNA, Y=Y chromosome, and S=segment). For example, DYS438 is a marker that has a certain number of repeats of the sequence "TTTTC." When DYS438 is tested, the testing company determines how many repeats of "TTTTC" are found at that location. A result of 7 for DYS438 would look like the following:

$$1 \quad\quad 2 \quad\quad 3 \quad\quad 4 \quad\quad 5 \quad\quad 6 \quad\quad 7$$
TTTTCTTTTCTTTTCTTTTCTTTTCTTTTCTTTTC

Occasionally, as the sequence is reproduced and passed down to the next generation, the number of repeats will randomly change, usually by a value of one or two. For example, the seven repeats in the sequence above might become six or eight. More rarely, the seven repeats might become five or nine.

The likelihood that two unrelated people will share the same number of repeats at multiple STR markers is low; that likelihood becomes progressively lower as additional STR markers are tested. For this reason, most genetic genealogists recommend testing a minimum of 37 markers, and preferably testing 67 or 111 markers.

In table 1, results are shown for 12 STR markers.[2] This collection of STR results is the test-taker's haplotype, the set of markers inherited by him, which will exactly match or be very similar to those of his close relatives. The more distant the relationship between two males, the more different their haplotypes will be.

Table 1. Y-DNA test results on 12 markers

Marker	DYS393	DYS390	DYS19	DYS391	DYS385	DYS426	DYS388	DYS439	DYS389I	DYS392	DYS389II
Value	13	25	13	10	17-18	11	12	12	13	11	30

For example, table 2 shows the Y-DNA test results on 12 markers for two males, Ugo and Henri, who are likely closely related. They differ at one marker, DYS391. At 12 markers, their Y-DNA genetic distance is 1. Y-DNA genetic distance is the number of differences between two Y-DNA haplotypes.

Table 2. Y-DNA test results on 12 markers for two men who are likely closely related

Marker	DYS393	DYS390	DYS19	DYS391	DYS385	DYS426	DYS388	DYS439	DYS389I	DYS392	DYS389II
Ugo	13	25	13	*10*	17-18	11	12	12	13	11	30
Henri	13	25	13	*9*	17-18	11	12	12	13	11	30

In contrast, table 3 shows the Y-DNA test results on 12 markers for two males, Kyle and Roy, who are not closely related. They have a genetic distance of six at 12 markers. They differ at only four markers, but the genetic distance is the total of all the differences between the two haplotypes.

---

[2] Some markers are called "multi-copy STR markers," meaning that there are multiple versions of the same STR in different locations on the Y chromosome. DYS385 is one example of a multi-copy STR marker, and thus two different values are shown in the results for that marker.

**Table 3. Y-DNA test results on 12 markers for two men
who are not closely related**

Marker	DYS393	DYS390	DYS19	DYS391	DYS385	DYS426	DYS388	DYS439	DYS389I	DYS392	DYS389II
Kyle	13	25	*13*	*9*	17-18	11	12	*11*	13	*11*	30
Roy	13	25	*12*	*11*	17-18	11	12	*12*	13	*9*	30

Y-STR Testing and Analysis

Family Tree DNA (https://www.familytreedna.com) has been doing Y-STR testing since 2000. It has the largest Y-STR database in the world. The company offers a variety of Y-STR tests, with the most popular being those that test 37, 67, and 111 markers. After Family Tree DNA obtains the test results (approximately four to six weeks on average), the company performs several analyses with the results.

Sample Y-STR results from Family Tree DNA are shown in figure 4. For each Y-STR marker, the marker name and the test-taker's result is shown. For example, this test-taker has a value of 13 at DYS393.

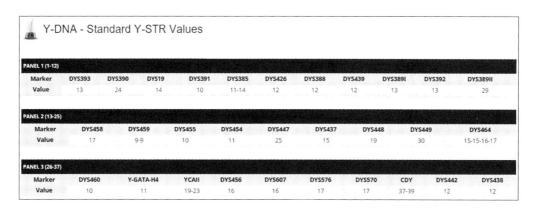

Figure 4. Sample Y-STR results from Family Tree DNA

The test-taker's Y-STR haplotype is then compared to every other Y-STR haplotype in the database, and a list of genetic matches above a certain threshold is returned. At 12 markers, for example, only exact matches are reported.[3] The thresholds for each of the testing levels are shown in table 4.

---

[3] Matches with a genetic distance of one will be shown for 12-marker tests if the matches belong to the same Y-DNA project as the test-taker.

Table 4. Thresholds for reporting a match at various testing levels

No. of markers compared	Maximum genetic distance at which a match will be reported
12	0
25	2
37	4
67	7
111	10

If the test-taker has one or more matches within the genetic-distance thresholds, the matches page at Family Tree DNA will look similar to figure 5. For the test-taker in figure 5, the closest match is Joshua J. Layne, with a genetic distance of two. Joshua J. Layne lists his most distant paternal ancestor, William Layne, born in England in 1752.

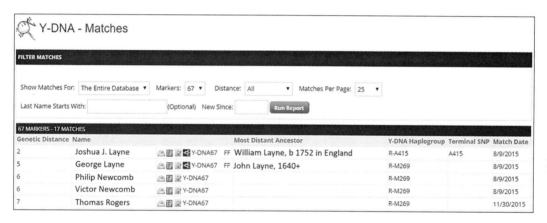

Figure 5. Sample Y-STR matches from Family Tree DNA

Genetic distance can be used to estimate the relationship of two test-takers. For example, table 5, adapted from information provided by Family Tree DNA,[4] categorizes the relationship between two men based on their genetic distance. These are approximations only; due to the randomness of Y-DNA, actual relationships and distances can vary. In rare instances, two or more random mutations may occur between father and son. Genetic genealogists are studying this phenomenon to determine the frequency at which this happens.

---

[4] "Expected Relationships with Y-DNA STR Matches," Family Tree DNA, *Family Tree DNA Learning Center BETA* (https://www.familytreedna.com/learn/y-dna-testing/y-str/expected-relationship-match/).

Table 5. Estimated category of relationship between two men based on Y-DNA

	Y-DNA Genetic Distance				
Relationship	12 markers	25 markers	37 markers	67 markers	111 markers
Very Closely Related	N/A	N/A	0	0	0
Closely Related	N/A	N/A	1	1–2	1–2
Related	0	0–1	2–3	3–4	3–5
Distantly Related	1	2	4	5–6	6–7
Very Distantly Related	≥2	≥3	≥5	≥7	≥8–10

Family Tree DNA also calculates genetic distance and estimates the number of generations to the most recent common patrilineal ancestor using a proprietary algorithm called Family Tree DNA's Time Predictor (FTDNATiP). FTDNATiP determines how closely two matches are related using mutation rates specific to each STR marker. FTDNATiP is accessed by clicking the icon labeled "TiP" next to each genetic match, as shown in figure 6.

67 MARKERS - 17 MATCHES
Genetic Distance Name
2   Joshua J. Layne   Y-DNA67   FF

Figure 6. The FTDNATiP calculator icon (circled)

The FTDNATiP calculator provides a probability of the number of generations to the most recent common patrilineal ancestor. In the example shown in figure 7, Harold Thompson Lane and Joshua J. Layne have a genetic distance of two, and the FTDNATiP calculator estimates a very strong probability (96.58 percent) that the men have a common ancestor somewhere within the past twelve generations.

The FTDNATiP calculator also allows the test-taker to refine the prediction with information from his family tree. For example, if Harold Thompson Lane knows that he is not related to Joshua J. Layne within the past five generations, he can recalculate the estimate after providing that information in the box on the TiP calculator page.

If the genetic match has agreed to share his test results, or if he has made them available via a DNA project, the test-taker can compare his results to his genetic match to determine the exact differences between their respective Y-DNA haplotypes. Figure 8, for example, is a screenshot of the results page of a Y-DNA surname project. Each of the participants of this surname project can compare their results to the other members to determine exactly how their haplotypes differ.

Y-DNA TiP Report

In comparing Y-DNA 67 marker results, the probability that **Mr. Harold Thompson Lane** and **Mr. Joshua J. Layne** shared a common ancestor within the last...

COMPARISON CHART	
Generations	**Percentage**
4	44.43%
8	84.11%
12	96.58%
16	99.37%
20	99.89%
24	99.98%

Refine your results with paper trail input

If traditional genealogical records indicate that a common ancestor between you and your match could not have lived in a certain number of past generations, your TiP results can be refined. Note, if you are not sure of this information, you should not change the value of "1" below.

Mr. Harold Thompson Lane and **Mr. Joshua J. Layne** did not share a common ancestor in the last [1] generation(s).

Markers [67 ▾] Display [every 4 generations. ▾] [RECALCULATE]

Figure 7. Sample FTDNATiP calculator page

Notably, several of the markers—DYS385, DYS439, and DYS458—are shaded. This indicates they are fast-moving markers (identified as mutating faster than others). Typically, fewer generations are needed for mutations to accumulate in fast-moving markers. Two men who differ only at two fast-moving markers may reasonably conclude that they are likely more closely related than two men who differ only at two slower-moving markers. The FTDNATiP calculator takes the slightly faster mutation rates of these markers into account when performing an analysis.

Markers: [Y-DNA12 ▾] Page Size: [500] ☑ Show All Columns

Kit Number	Name	Paternal Ancestor Name	Country	Haplogroup	DYS393	DYS390	DYS19	DYS391	DYS385	DYS426	DYS388	DYS439	DYS389i	DYS392	DYS389ii	DYS458	DYS459
Ungrouped																	
128391	Bettinger		Ukraine	J-M172	12	23	15	10	13-18	11	15	11	12	11	28	17	8-9
57020	Bettinger	Philip Bettinger, b 1752 in Germany	Germany	R-A415	13	24	14	10	11-14	12	12	12	13	13	29	17	9-9
368390	Bettinger		Germany	R-M269	13	24	14	10	11-14	12	12	12	13	13	29	17	9-9
186827	Ettinger	Oettingen	Austria	R-M512	13	25	16	10	11-14	12	12	10	13	11	30	14	9-10
H1218	Barrett-Bettcher	Michael Boettcher, b1794, d1855 Bessarabia	Poland	R-Z283	13	25	17	10	10-14	12	12	10	14	11	32	16	9-10
200802	Bettinger	Philip Bettinger, b.1833 and d. 1908	Germany	I-L39	14	25	17	11	13-14	11	13	11	12	11	28	16	8-10

Figure 8. Screenshot of the results page of a Y-DNA surname project

Adoption and Misattributed Parentage

Males who do not have information about their genetic heritage due to adoption, misattributed parentage, or some other reason, can use Y-STR testing to potentially identify a surname and find close paternal matches. Because the Y chromosome is so closely associated with surnames, a male may pass down information about his surname to his biological child—even if the child does not know the surname.

In figure 9, for example, the adopted test-taker has no information about his biological surname. He ordered a 67-marker test from Family Tree DNA in the hopes of finding a close match who could potentially shed light on the surname. In this extreme example, the test-taker received a very strong clue that his biological surname may be O'Shea or a close variant.

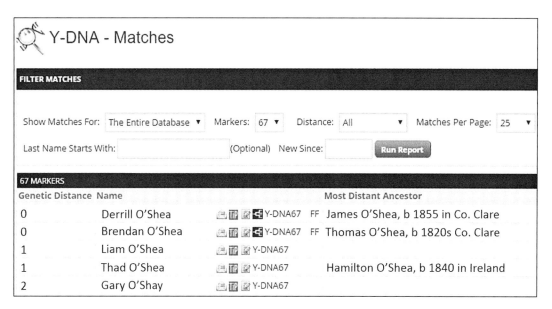

Figure 9. Y-STR matches page at Family Tree DNA

It is important to remember that this is only a clue. Additional sources would have to be examined, such as atDNA testing and documentary evidence. It is possible, for example, that while the test-taker's biological surname may have been O'Shea within the past few generations, other misattributed-parentage events may have resulted in his biological father, grandfather, or other generations having a different surname. It is not unusual for multiple generations in one family to have misattributed parentage.

In addition to Family Tree DNA's database, the public database called *Ysearch* (http://www.ysearch.org) can be mined for genetic matches. *Ysearch* was created and is supported by Family Tree DNA. While the vast majority of the matches are from Family Tree DNA (approximately 88 percent), the very large database—approaching 200,000 records—contains results from thousands of individuals who tested at other companies. Using *Ysearch* is often the only way to identify those matches.

2. Y-DNA SNPs

Single nucleotide polymorphisms, or SNPs (pronounced "snips"), are variations in a single nucleotide of a person's entire DNA. For example, a SNP may be a cytosine (C) in some people while it is a thymine (T) in other people. Since SNPs are usually inherited from the previous generation, they can be used to examine relatedness between two or more individuals.

Y-SNP tests examine anywhere between one and thousands of SNPs located all along the Y chromosome. A Y-SNP test result will indicate that at that marker the test-taker is either

- ancestral (also called negative, indicated by a "−" sign), meaning that the test-taker and his ancestors have not mutated at that location, or that he has back-mutated at that SNP;[5] or
- derived (also called positive, indicated by a "+" sign), meaning that the test-taker has a mutation at that SNP.

Most people do not typically start out with SNP testing, but it may be recommended after Y-STR testing as a way to further define a test-taker's haplogroup. Indeed, a SNP test has several important uses, including determining the haplogroup and learning about ancient ancestry of the paternal line.

Using the results of a SNP test, the testing company will place the test-taker on a particular branch of the human Y-DNA haplogroup tree. This is accomplished by determining the test-taker's terminal SNP (the Y-SNP that defines the most distant branch of the human family tree for which the test-taker has tested). The International Society of Genetic Genealogy (ISOGG) maintains a Y-SNP index (http://www.isogg.org/tree/ISOGG_YDNA_SNP_Index.html) as well as a detailed Y-DNA haplogroup tree (http://www.isogg.org/tree/index.html).

For example, J-M67 is a terminal SNP in Y-DNA haplogroup J. It corresponds to the older haplogroup designation J2a1b. J-M67 is abundant in the Caucasus, Italy, and on the Iberian Peninsula. This sub-clade (a sub-branch of the human tree) of Y-DNA haplogroup J is estimated to have originated approximately nine thousand to twelve thousand years ago. The results for a test-taker with terminal SNP J-M67 might look like this:

Haplogroup	SNP Results	Terminal SNP
J2a1b	M172+ M410+ L26+ M47+ M67+ M68−	J-M67

Each of the SNPs in the results helps place the test-taker on the Y-DNA haplogroup J tree. For example, the first SNP result, M172+, indicates the test-taker is derived at the SNP called M172, which is a characteristic SNP for Y-DNA haplogroup J. The test-taker is also derived at M410, L26, M47, and M67, but is ancestral at M68. Using the Y-DNA

---

[5] A back mutation occurs when a SNP mutates to a derived value, then mutates again, returning to the ancestral value.

haplogroup J tree provided by ISOGG—a portion of which is reproduced below—the most distant branch to which the test-taker can be mapped is J-M67:

J2 M172		Derived
J2a M410		Derived
J2a1 L26, L27		Derived
J2a1a M47		Derived
J2a1b M67		Derived
J2a1c M68		Ancestral

Thus, the test-taker's Y-DNA belongs to haplogroup J, sub-clade J2a1b, because he is derived for the M67 SNP but is ancestral for the M68 SNP.

Since haplogroups are defined by SNP mutations, the Y-STR testing described above can only provide an estimate of a test-taker's haplogroup. This estimate can be verified with Y-SNP testing. If an estimate is available based on Y-STR testing, Y-SNP testing can often be focused rather than broad spectrum. In figure 10, for example, the test-taker is estimated to belong to Y-DNA haplogroup E-L117 or one of its branches or sub-clades, of which there are many. The SNPs in this predicted haplogroup tree are color-coded for any that are Tested Positive, Tested Negative, Presumed Positive, Test Available, Presumed Negative, and Test in Progress. In the color version of figure 10, all the SNPs shown above E-L117 (for example, P177, P179, and M215) are coded as Presumed Positive, while all those below E-L117 (for example, V68 and L541) are coded as Test Available.

Figure 10. Y-DNA haplogroup estimate from Family Tree DNA

If the test-taker has results from SNP testing, the haplogroup tree assignment will be verified, as shown in figure 11. This test-taker has tested positive for S11515, L1, A415, and S1791 in this tree, and his verified haplogroup is R-A415.

After the test-taker has information about his haplogroup, either estimated or confirmed, he can research the haplogroup to learn more about the ancient origins of his patrilineal line. Most haplogroups are associated with a particular region and time, and some are associated with a specific ethnic or biogeographical group. Males with Native American ancestry on their paternal line, for example, typically belong to a sub-clade of either haplogroup Q-M242 or haplogroup C-P39.

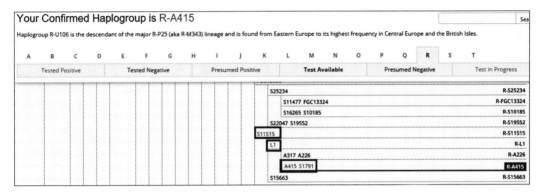

Figure 11. Y-DNA haplogroup confirmation from Family Tree DNA

Large-Scale Y-SNP Projects

Traditional Y-DNA SNP tests examine between one and thousands of SNPs located all along the Y chromosome. However, new tests are examining more markers and identifying new SNPs that may be useful in a genealogically relevant timeframe. These so-called "family SNPs" are mutations that developed recently and only had time to propagate within the past one hundred to two hundred years. Table 6 identifies several large-scale Y-SNP tests available to genetic genealogists,

Table 6. Large-scale Y-SNP tests

	Genographic Project 2.0	BritainsDNA Chromo2	Family Tree DNA BigY	Full Genomes
Type	Chip	Chip	Sequencing	Sequencing
Number of SNPs	19,000+	14,400+	25,000–35,000	50,000–55,000
Novel SNPs?	No	No	Yes	Yes

The BigY test at Family Tree DNA was created to sequence large portions of a test-taker's Y chromosome to identify new SNPs that could further refine the human Y-DNA haplogroup tree. The test sequences approximately eleven million bases of the Y chromosome, with a high level of confidence, identifying any novel SNPs that may be contained within this region. The sequencing identifies between 25,000 and 35,000 SNPs, many of which are not yet placed on the human Y-DNA tree. These novel SNPs will play an important role in defining the Y-DNA family tree and in refining knowledge about relationships in a genealogically relevant timeframe. The new SNPs will be placed on the Y-DNA family tree as they are associated with haplogroups and sub-clades, and tools will allow test-takers to use the new SNPs to refine or establish MRCA calculations.

Soon after releasing the first results of BigY testing, Family Tree DNA began to perform matching using the results. In the next few years, Y-STR and Y-SNP tests will increasingly be used together to examine relatedness and to answer genealogical questions.

Chapter 3 Exercises

Use the family tree chart titled "Descendants of Thomas and Sarah (Underhill) Chrisman" to answer questions 1, 2, and 3. The genealogist has confirmed that there are no known common ancestors for the people on the chart other than those shown. Each kinship link has been confirmed with strong documentary evidence.

Hint: The easiest way to answer these questions is to make a copy of the chart, then, beginning with Thomas Chrisman, use a unique mark to identify all descendants who may have inherited Y-DNA from him.

Descendants of Thomas and Sarah (Underhill) Chrisman

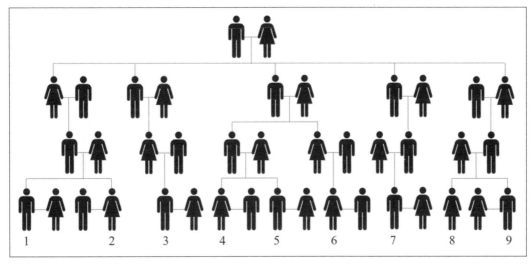

1. Which of the descendants in the bottom row (the great-grandchildren) may have inherited the Y-DNA of their great-grandfather Thomas Chrisman?

_____

_____

_____

2. How many men in the family tree may have inherited their Y-DNA from Thomas Chrisman? Do not include Thomas in the count.

_____

_____

_____

3. Thomas Chrisman had three sons, each of whom has grandsons of his own. Is there a grandson in each of the three sons' lines who may have inherited Thomas Chrisman's Y-DNA? Why or why not?

_____

_____

_____

Use the family tree chart titled "Descendants of Lawrence and Diana (?) Richmond" to answer questions 4 and 5.

Descendants of Lawrence and Diana (?) Richmond

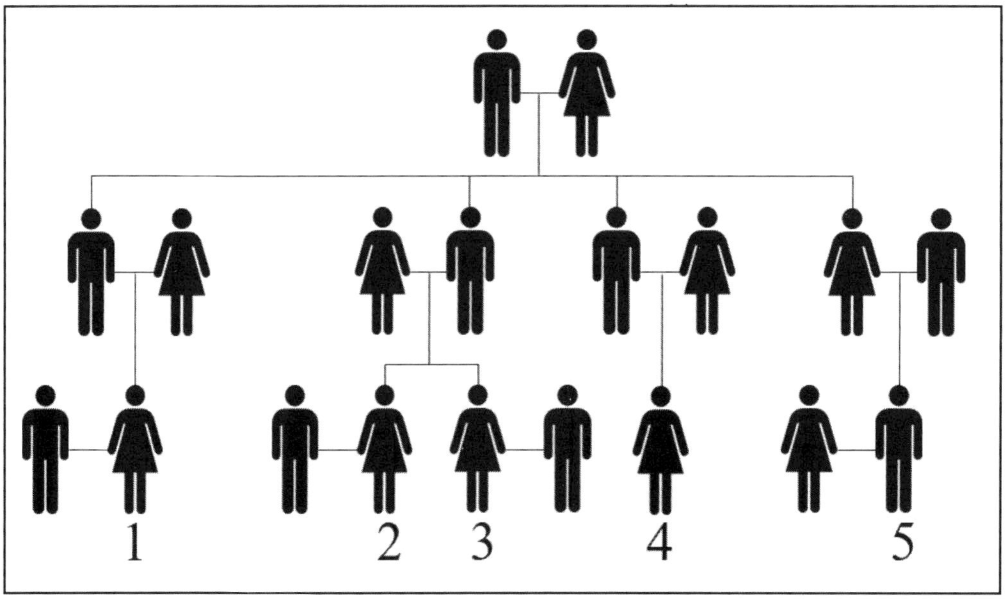

4. Which of the five grandchildren in this chart (numbered 1–5) may have inherited their Y-DNA from their grandfather Lawrence Richmond?

_____

_____

_____

5. Based on the answer to question 4, what is the next step in examining the Y-DNA of grandfather Lawrence Richmond?

_____

_____

_____

Additional research going back a generation uncovers the names of Lawrence Richmond's parents, Hiram and Susannah (Lyon) Richmond. Research also uncovers descendants of two of Lawrence Richmond's three brothers. Using the extended tree titled "Descendants of Hiram and Susannah (Lyon) Richmond," answer questions 6 and 7.

Descendants of Hiram and Susannah (Lyon) Richmond

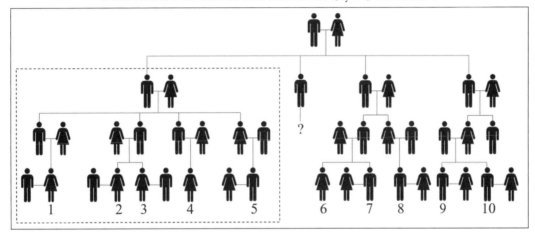

6. Hiram Richmond has ten living great-grandchildren (numbered 1–10). Circle everyone in the tree who should possess the Richmond family Y-DNA. Which of the great-grandchildren inherited their Y-DNA from Hiram Richmond?

_____

_____

_____

7. If the male great-grandchild(ren) in this descendancy chart decline to take a Y-DNA test, what other Y-DNA testing strategy could a genealogist pursue to learn about the Richmond family's Y-DNA?

_____

_____

_____

Use the family tree chart titled "Descendants of John and Jane [?] Albro" to answer questions 8 through 13. For some questions, it may be easiest to create a table showing the marker values for each test-taker and the path back to John Albro. To determine which markers are fast moving, the Y-DNA quick-reference notes available on Debbie Parker Wayne's blog, *Deb's Delvings in Genealogy* (http://debs-delvings.blogspot.com/search/label/QuickRef), may be helpful.

Descendants of John and Jane (?) Albro

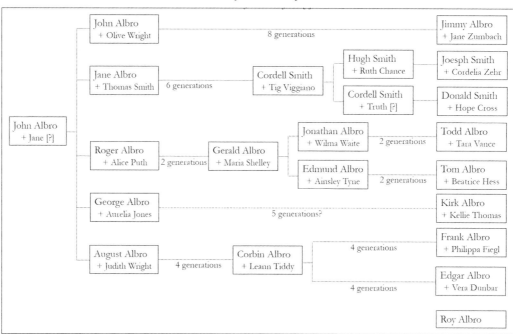

Genealogist Roy Albro has constructed a family tree containing all known descendants of John and Jane [?] Albro of New Hampshire, numbering in the thousands. Roy believes he fits in the tree somewhere, but documentary research has not definitively placed him.

With a goal of finding additional clues, Roy tested himself and eight known descendants of John Albro using a SNP-based test from the testing company 23andMe (which provides the Y-DNA haplogroup) and a 37-marker Y-DNA test from Family Tree DNA. The combined results are provided in the following table.

	23andMe Paternal Haplogroup	DYS393	DYS390	DYS319	DYS391	DYS385	DYS426	DYS388	DYS439	DYS389i	DYS392	DYS389ii	DYS458	DYS459	DYS455	DYS454	DYS447	DYS437	DYS448	DYS449
Jimmy Albro	R1b1b2	13	24	14	10	11-14	12	12	13	13	13	29	17	9-9	10	11	25	15	19	31
Joseph Smith	R1b1b2	13	24	14	11	11-14	12	12	12	13	13	29	18	9-10	11	11	25	15	19	29
Donald Smith	R1b1b2	13	24	14	11	11-14	12	12	12	13	13	29	18	9-10	11	11	25	15	19	29
Todd Albro	R1b1b2	13	24	14	10	11-14	12	12	12	13	13	29	17	9-9	10	11	25	15	19	30
Tom Albro	R1b1b2	13	24	14	10	11-14	12	12	12	13	13	29	17	9-9	10	11	25	15	19	30
Kirk Albro	R1b1b2	13	24	14	10	11-14	12	12	13	13	13	29	17	9-9	10	11	26	15	19	30
Frank Albro	R1b1b2	13	24	14	10	11-14	12	12	12	13	13	29	17	9-9	10	11	25	15	19	30
Edgar Albro	E1b1b1a	13	23	13	10	15-16	11	12	12	13	11	31	17	9-9	12	11	25	14	20	33
Roy Albro	R1b1b2	13	24	14	10	11-14	12	12	13	13	13	29	17	9-9	10	11	26	15	19	30

	DYS464	DYS460	GATA-H4	YCAII	DYS456	DYS607	DYS576	DYS570	CDY	DYS442	DYS438	DYS531	DYS578	DYF395S1	DYS590	DYS537	DYS641	DYS472
Jimmy Albro	15-15-16-17	10	11	19-23	16	16	16	17	37-39	12	12	11	9	15-16	8	10	10	8
Joseph Smith	15-16-17-18	11	10	19-23	16	16	17	17	36-37	11	12	11	9	15-16	8	10	10	8
Donald Smith	15-16-17-18	11	10	19-23	16	16	17	17	36-37	11	12	11	9	15-16	8	10	10	8
Todd Albro	15-15-16-17	10	11	19-23	16	16	17	17	37-39	12	12	11	9	15-16	8	10	10	8
Tom Albro	15-15-16-17	10	11	19-23	16	16	17	17	37-39	12	12	11	9	15-16	8	10	10	8
Kirk Albro	15-15-16-17	10	11	19-23	16	16	17	18	37-39	12	12	11	9	15-16	8	10	10	8
Frank Albro	15-15-16-17	10	11	19-23	16	16	17	17	37-39	12	12	11	9	15-16	8	10	10	8
Edgar Albro	14-15-15-17	11	11	19-22	15	12	18	18	37-37	13	10	10	8	15-17	8	11	10	8
Roy Albro	15-15-16-17	10	11	19-23	16	16	17	18	37-39	12	12	11	9	15-16	8	10	10	8

8. Based **solely** on the 23andMe paternal haplogroup listed in the second column, could the reconstructed family tree for Jimmy Albro, Todd Albro, Tom Albro, Kirk Albro, Frank Albro, and Edgar Albro be correct?

_____

_____

_____

9. What could explain Edgar Albro's Y-DNA test results?

_____

_____

_____

10. Should Joseph Smith and Donald Smith share the same Y-DNA as the Albro males? Why or why not?

_____

_____

_____

11. Do Joseph Smith and Donald Smith share the same Y-DNA as the Albro males?

_____

_____

_____

12. Looking at only the results for Jimmy, Todd, Tom, Kirk, and Frank Albro, map the Y-DNA mutations to the family tree. Do the DNA results correlate logically with the family tree? Can you identify the places in the family tree where the mutations on markers DYS439, 447, 576, and 570 likely occurred?

_____

_____

_____

13. Could Roy fit within this Albro family tree based on the results of the Y-DNA testing? Based on the results, where might he fit best?

_____

_____

_____

Walter believes his great-grandfather had Native American ancestry on the paternal line. He orders a 37-marker Y-DNA test from Family Tree DNA. Based on the results, Walter's estimated haplogroup is R1b1b2a.

14. Based on the DNA test results, is Walter's Y chromosome Native American? Could Walter's great-grandfather have had Native American ancestry on his paternal line?

_____

_____

_____

Luther orders a 67-marker Y-STR test from Family Tree DNA. The company predicts his haplogroup to be R. Luther orders a SNP test to further refine his placement on haplogroup R, and he receives the following results:

> M207+, M173+, M343+, P297+, M269+, L23+, L51+, L151+, U106+, S263+,
> Z301+, L146−, Z156−

15. Using the 2015 version of the ISOGG Y-DNA Haplogroup R Tree (http://isogg.org/tree/ISOGG_HapgrpR15.html) and Luther's Y-SNP results, determine Luther's terminal SNP.

_____

_____

_____

Jason is adopted and searching for information about his genetic heritage. He orders a 67-marker Y-DNA test from Family Tree DNA and receives his results eight weeks later. Jason has six matches at 67 markers, including five matches at a genetic distance of three or closer.

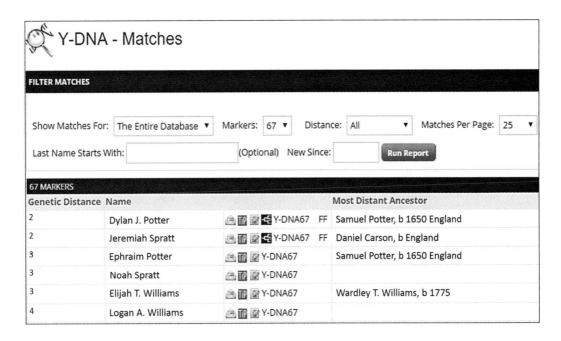

16. Can Jason make any conclusions about his biological surname based on his Y-DNA matches?

_____

_____

_____

Genealogical Applications for mtDNA

What is mtDNA?

Mitochondrial DNA (mtDNA) is located in each cell, outside of the cell's nucleus. Almost every cell in our bodies contains hundreds to thousands of copies of the mtDNA molecule. Some companies test a few mtDNA locations as part of an atDNA test, but to use mtDNA for genealogical purposes, a separate mtDNA test provides the best results.

A mother's egg contains mtDNA, which is passed down from the mother to all of her children. Only her daughters will pass mtDNA to the next generation. Men have mtDNA, but they do not pass it down to their children. A child, therefore, inherits mtDNA only from his or her mother.

Although there are multiple copies of mitochondria in each of our cells, mtDNA does not recombine before being passed to the next generation. Random mutations can occur as mtDNA is copied, but otherwise it is passed unchanged and without recombination.

Mutations in mtDNA occur rarely. As a result, two people who match on every mtDNA location may have a recent common mtDNA ancestor, or may have a common mtDNA ancestor so far back in time that no documentary evidence exists to support the link.

The mtDNA molecule is circular. If the circle were cut and untwisted it would look like a ladder, just as all DNA does. The mtDNA molecule is small compared to nuclear DNA. It is about 16,569 locations in length. The exact length varies depending on whether mutations have resulted in additions or deletions.

mtDNA Inheritance Patterns

The path through which mtDNA is passed is often referred to as a person's matrilineal line. In the pedigree chart in figure 1 the matrilineal line is shaded.

In figure 2, the mtDNA inheritance is shown in a descendancy chart. Circles represent women and squares represent men. The top row represents a couple. Children of the couple, one son and two daughters, are shown on the second row, along with their mates. The third row shows grandchildren and their mates. Row four shows great-grand-children. A female passes her mtDNA to all of her children, but a male does not pass his mtDNA to his children. Because of this unique inheritance pattern, only the family members with an "m" in the circle or square will have the mtDNA passed down from the woman in the top row. If only those on the bottom row are still living, there are only two potential mtDNA test-takers in this family for questions related to the mtDNA of the woman at the top.

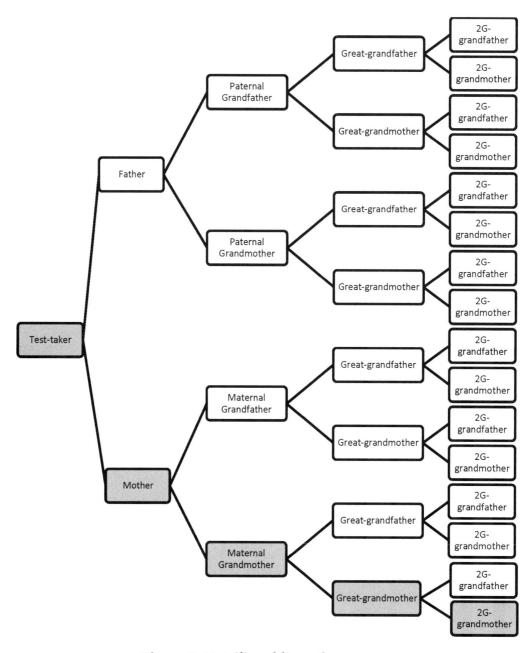

Figure 1. Matrilineal line of ancestors

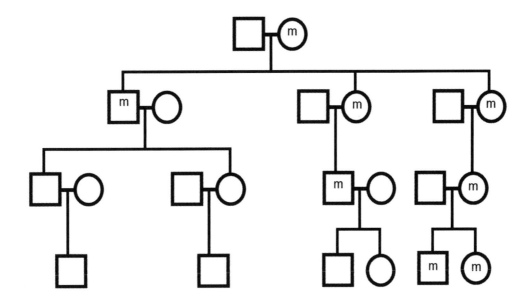

Figure 2. Matrilineal line of descendants

Advantages and Limitations for mtDNA

The unique inheritance pattern of mtDNA offers both advantages and limitations when considering mtDNA for use in a genealogical problem. The lack of recombination means the same mtDNA footprint will be passed down for many generations (except on the rare occasion when a mutation occurs). This allows a line to be traced many generations back in time. The relatively low rate of mtDNA mutations most often results in all of a woman's descendants in the mtDNA-inheritance line sharing the exact same DNA for hundreds of years or more.

Having the same mtDNA footprint passed down for many generations is a major advantage when trying to determine if a matrilineal line was of a specific biogeographical origin, such as African or Native American.[1] The origin-identifying markers will not be diluted by recombination and will persist through all generations. Another advantage to testing mtDNA is that a significant mismatch can definitively rule out a relationship on the matrilineal line.

The same characteristics that make mtDNA useful in some situations make it difficult to work with in others. It is impossible to determine, for example, which of a woman's daughters or granddaughters is the ancestor of a particular line of descendants. An exact mtDNA match provides evidence of a common ancestor, while not helping to identify which woman in that matrilineal line is that common ancestor. Recent or rare mutations shared by two mtDNA test-takers may help prove a recent matrilineal relationship,

---

[1] While mtDNA can indicate Native American ancestry on the matrilineal line, it usually cannot determine which tribe a person may have been part of.

however the rarity of such mutations means only a few people will be lucky enough to find this evidence in their family's DNA.

Test Strategies for mtDNA

Genealogical questions that mtDNA may be able to help answer include (1) whether a matrilineal line descends from a specific ethnic or biogeographical origin, such as African or Native American; (2) whether it is possible that two woman were in the same matrilineal line; and (3) from which of two women (not related through their matrilineal lines) a person descends. After establishing that mtDNA may help answer a question, it is necessary to identify which descendants can be tested and to determine the required test resolution.

Descendant family trees will be needed to trace a matrilineal line to determine if there is a living person who can be asked to take an mtDNA test. A speculative tree can be drawn by hand or created in a software program to track the focus woman's known descendants. Starting with the focus mtDNA ancestor, each descendant who inherited mtDNA from that woman should be marked. The marked living descendants can be asked to take an mtDNA test. If there are no living descendants in the matrilineal line, or a living descendant is not willing to test, it may be necessary to research back a generation to see if the focus ancestor had sisters who have living descendants in the matrilineal line. If no test candidate is found, it may be necessary to research back another generation to see if the focus ancestor had maternal aunts who have living descendants in the matrilineal line. Because mtDNA is passed down without recombination, it is possible to research back many generations in the search for potential mtDNA test-takers.

mtDNA Tests

In the early days of genetic genealogy, low-resolution mtDNA tests were offered at a fairly high cost compared to Y-DNA tests. Prices have decreased over the years, while knowledge of the usefulness of all types of DNA has increased. For example, Family Tree DNA once offered low- and medium-resolution tests as well as the full mtDNA sequence. Only the medium-resolution and full sequence tests are now offered as the low resolution test is unable to answer most genealogical questions. Before ordering a test, it is important to check with a testing company to determine exactly how much of the mtDNA molecule will be sequenced. Current posts on genetic-genealogy blogs and in the *ISOGG Wiki* (http://www.isogg.org/wiki) may provide the most up-to-date information on available tests and their coverage.

Low- and medium-resolution mtDNA tests can determine whether a matrilineal line is of a specific ethnic or biogeographical origin, such as African or Native American, or may indicate two matrilineal lines are not related. These tests focus on segments where mutations seem to cluster. The segments are called hyper-variable regions (HVR) or hyper-variable segments (HVS). Some companies divide the HVR into two segments; some companies divide the same general area into three segments. Testing companies may use different start and stop locations for the segments, even if the companies label the segments the same way (HVR1, for example). This must be remembered when analyzing mtDNA data that is not from a full-sequence test. One company might identify a mutation that is not listed by a second company only because the second company did not test that specific location—even if both companies indicate the HVR1 segment, for example, was tested. After analyzing results from a low- or medium-resolution test, it may be necessary to upgrade to the higher-resolution test to obtain better evidence.

The full mitochondrial sequence, which is generally the most useful for genealogy, tests every location in the mtDNA molecule. No further test upgrades will be needed after the full sequence is performed. The test includes all HVR as well as the coding region (CR), which is a region that contains DNA that can include medically significant information about the test-taker. Test-takers who are concerned about revealing health-related information should have the data analyzed by someone who understands the potential medical significance prior to sharing results about the CR.

Figure 3 shows an mtDNA molecule with start and stop locations that may be used to define different segments. The exact start and stop locations may be defined differently by each testing company. The segment divisions shown are those used by Family Tree DNA.

An exact match even on a full-sequence mtDNA test may only indicate two people have a common ancestor in the last five to twenty or so generations; the mtDNA test may not narrow the number of generations down to a small number, as can sometimes be done with a Y-DNA test.

It can be difficult to trace women in cultures where surnames changed at marriage and where women had little legal standing. Many genealogists have blanks where the women should be named in their family trees. Without a complete and accurate family tree that includes women, mtDNA evidence is difficult to incorporate into genealogical research. Despite the limitations, there are some genealogical questions where an mtDNA test is the only DNA test that will provide essential evidence.

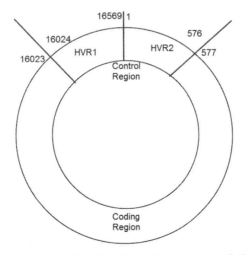

**Figure 3. mtDNA molecule showing regional divisions,
as defined by Family Tree DNA**

mtDNA Test Results

Low-resolution mtDNA tests generally include only HVR1. Medium-resolution mtDNA tests generally include both HVR1 and HVR2 segments of the mtDNA molecule. These tests determine the basic mtDNA haplogroup—the main branch of the mtDNA tree—a person belongs to. The tests also provide a list of differences between the tested DNA and a reference sequence.

The Cambridge Reference Sequence (CRS) was the original mtDNA sequence published in 1981.[2] A revision, published in 1999,[3] corrected eleven errors. That revision is now often referred to as the CRS, although more correctly it is referenced as the Revised Cambridge Reference Sequence (rCRS). Experienced researchers use the corrected sequence.

There is nothing special about the CRS except that it was the first full mitochondrial sequence published for humans. It does not represent the root of the mtDNA haplogroup tree. Because of this, some scientists reconstructed a likely reference sequence for that root; it is called the Reconstructed Sapiens Reference Sequence (RSRS).[4] The reconstructed sequence allows a comparison of a test-taker's mtDNA results to what is believed to be the mtDNA sequence of the earliest human ancestor of all living people.

The most commonly used reference sequence is the rCRS. Some companies and tools also provide a comparison to the RSRS. The two sequences (CRS/rCRS and RSRS) should not be compared to one another for genealogical purposes. When analyzing mtDNA results, it is always necessary to use the same reference sequence comparison for all test-takers.

Shorthand references are typically used to indicate the state of each mtDNA location. A number indicates the tested location (the rung of the ladder or the base pair tested); it is followed by an A, G, C, or T to indicate the chemical sequenced at that location (for example, 150T). In some lists, a letter preceding the number indicates the value of the location in the reference sequence (for example, C150T). A deletion (represented by a "D" or a "–") indicates an expected value at the location is missing from the tested person (for example, 4977D). An addition, represented by a period followed by a number, indicates there is DNA inserted at that location. A ".1" indicates a single base pair insertion following the indicated location, a .2 indicates a second base pair insertion, and so on (for example, 315.1C and 523.2A). The term indels is used to refer to both insertions and deletions. Back mutations (reversions to an ancestral state) are indicated with an exclamation point (for example, G16129A!). Double reversions are indicated with two exclamation points (for example, G15301A!!).

[2] S. Anderson et al., "Sequence and Organization of the Human Mitochondrial Genome," *Nature* 290 (9 April 1981): 457–65; digital images, *MitoMap* (http://www.mitomap.org/pub/MITOMAP/MitoSeqs/Anderson1981CRS.pdf).

[3] R. Andrews et al., "Reanalysis and Revision of the Cambridge Reference Sequence for Human Mitochondrial DNA," *Nature Genetics* 23 (1999): 147.

[4] D. Behar et al., "A 'Copernican' Reassessment of the Human Mitochondrial DNA Tree from its Root," *The American Journal of Human Genetics* 90 (April 2012): 675–84; archived at National Center for BioTechnology Information, *PubMed Central* (http://www.ncbi.nlm.nih.gov/pmc/articles/PMC3322232/); DOI: 10.1016/j.ajhg.2012.03.002.

The mtDNA test results for a low- or medium-resolution test may be similar to table 1. The low-resolution test returns only the HVR1 differences from a reference sample. The medium-resolution test returns the HVR1 and HVR2 differences. Both tests return a basic-level haplogroup (in this example, U5b). Family Tree DNA no longer offers tests for only HVR1.

Table 1. mtDNA low- and medium-resolution test results	
Haplogroup	**U5b**
HVR1 differences from rCRS	16192T, 16218T, 16270T, 16320T
HVR2 differences from rCRS	73G, 150T, 263G, 315.1C, 523.1C, 523.2A

A full mtDNA sequence usually provides a more detailed haplogroup designation (in this example, U5b1d1c), and a list of differences between the reference sample and HVR1, HVR2, and CR, as shown in table 2.

Table 2. Full mtDNA sequence test results	
Haplogroup	**U5b1d1c**
HVR1 differences from rCRS	16192T, 16218T, 16270T, 16320T
HVR2 differences from rCRS	73G, 150T, 263G, 315.1C, 523.1C, 523.2A
Coding Region differences from rCRS	750G, 1438G, 2706G, 3197C, 4769G, 5437T, 5656G, 7028T, 7768G, 7912A, 8860G, 9477A, 11476G, 11719A, 12308G, 12372A, 13617C, 14182C, 14766T, 14326G, 15631G, 15721C

The raw data for a full mtDNA sequence is usually provided in a format known as FASTA, as shown in figure 4. The first line indicates the test kit number—123456—and the regions of mtDNA that were tested—HVR1, HVR2, and CR. Normal DNA data is represented by the letters GCAT. The FASTA file usually contains an N or a dash (–) as a placeholder at location 3107. This represents one correction the rCRS made to the CRS sequence. Letters other than GCAT or the N at 3107—for example, the R in figure 4—may indicate heteroplasmies. A heteroplasmy exists when some of the mitochondria may have different alleles (GCAT) at the same location than other mitochondria. This is discussed below. The dots represent lines that were removed from the file; the actual file consists of many more rows of values found at each of the approximately 16,569 rungs of the mtDNA ladder.

Figure 4. FASTA file

>123456,HVR2,CR,HVR1

GATCACAGGTCTATCACCCTATTAACCACTCACGGGAGCTCTCCATGCATTTGGTATTTTCGTC
TGGGGGGTGTGCACGC

…

TTGTTCAACGATTAAAGTCCTACGTGATCTGAGTTCAGACCGGAGTAATCCAGGTCGGTTTCT
ATCTA**N**CTTCAAATTCC

…

CTAAAGTGAACTGTATCCGACATCTGGTTCCTACTTCAGG**R**TCATAAAGCCTAAATAGCCCAC
ACGTTCCCCTTAAATAA

GACATCACGATG

Haplogroups

The testing company will interpret the mtDNA test results and place the test-taker on a particular branch of the human mtDNA haplogroup tree. This is accomplished by comparing the SNP values to branch-defining SNP values. *PhyloTree* (http://phylotree.org) maintains an mtDNA haplotree used by scientists and genetic genealogists. Some companies and third-party tools use different versions of the tree. This can result in slightly different haplogroup designations, depending on the version of the tree used.

The first letter of the haplogroup designates the main branch of the mtDNA tree to which a test-taker belongs. Subsequent letters and numbers provide a more defined haplogroup and place a test-taker on a sub-branch or sub-clade of the main haplogroup or clade.

The test-taker whose results are shown in table 2 is in mtDNA haplogroup U5b1d1c. Haplogroup U branched off from haplogroup R approximately forty-seven thousand years ago in west Asia. Descendants of this line migrated into Europe. Approximately thirty thousand years ago haplogroup U5 branched from U, and U5b branched off between four thousand and eighteen thousand years ago.[5] The subsequent sub-branches occurred in the years after U5b was founded.

The rCRS falls into haplogroup H2a2a1.[6] The values from a test-taker's full mtDNA sequence results can be used to trace the tree from the reference sequence up to a branching point then back down to the test-taker's haplogroup.

---

[5] National Geographic, *The Genographic Project* (https://genographic.national geographic.com), "mtDNA Your Map," anonymous test-taker no. NG3UBLY5V2.

[6] "Cambridge Reference Sequence," *ISOGG Wiki* (http://isogg.org/wiki/Cambridge_Reference_Sequence).

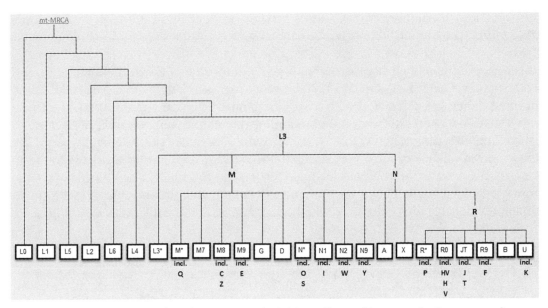

Figure 5. mtDNA haplotree at *PhyloTree* (http://www.phylotree.org)

Table 3 focuses on mutations that place a test-taker on the mtDNA haplogroup U tree and the most distant branch to which the test-taker can be mapped—U5b1d1c. Mutations at 309.1C and 315.1C as well as AC indels at 515–22, 16182C, 16183C, 16193.1C, and 16519, are typically excluded from the tree and are not included in this table.[7] Any differences from the reference sequence that are not haplogroup-defining mutations may be recent mutations that may be useful in a genealogically relevant timeframe.

Table 3. Example of mutations defining a haplogroup

Haplogroup	Defining mutations (showing ancestral and derived values)
U	A11467G, A12308G, G12372A
● U5	C16192T, C16270T
●● U5a'b	T3197C, G9477A, T13617C
●●● U5b	C150T, A7768G, T14182C
●●●● U5b1	A5656G
●●●●● U5b1d	C5437T
●●●●●● U5b1d1	T15721C
●●●●●●● U5b1d1c	G7912A, A15631G, C16218T, C16320T

---

[7] "PhyloTree.org—mtDNA tree Build 17 (18 Feb 2016)," *Phylotree* (http://phylotree.org/tree/index.htm).

The low- and medium-resolution tests provide a basic indication of a test-taker's haplogroup. The full mtDNA sequence can verify and further define the haplogroup.

Researching an identified haplogroup can reveal information about the ancient origins of a test-taker's matrilineal line. Most haplogroups are associated with a particular region and time. Some are associated with a specific ethnic or biogeographical group. Those with Native American ancestry on their matrilineal line, for example, typically belong to a sub-clade of haplogroups A, B, C, D, or X. Some sub-clades of these haplogroups are also found in other locations. For example, the mtDNA haplogroup D2a1a is found in Native Americans in the Aleutian Islands. Testing the full mtDNA sequence to get the most specific sub-clade designation, then correlating the mtDNA evidence with documentary evidence, helps determine whether a matrilineal line could be Native American.

Heteroplasmies

Many mitochondria exist in each cell. Due to mutation, some of the mitochondria may have different alleles (GCAT) at the same location than other mitochondria in the same cell or in other cells in the body. This is called a heteroplasmy. Heteroplasmies may persist across many generations.

Current testing procedures are sensitive enough to detect heteroplasmies when about 20 percent of the mitochondria have the mutated value.[8] Most companies report heteroplasmies using an ambiguity-code system adopted by the International Union of Pure and Applied Chemistry and described in a 1983 technical paper.[9] Family Tree DNA uses this nomenclature, as shown in table 4, to indicate the state of a heteroplasmy.

Hot Spots

Just as Y-DNA has fast-moving markers where mutations or differences are seen more often, mtDNA has hot spots, where frequent differences are seen or where the same DNA values are seen in multiple haplogroups. Companies and analysis tools vary in their interpretation of some or all of the differences, insertions, and deletions at locations 309, 315, around 522 (approximately 514 to 524), 16182, 16183, 16193, and 16519.[10] Reporting these hot spot locations as differences can significantly affect the interpretation of mtDNA results. It is important to determine whether the testing company or tool you use

---

[8] Ann Turner, "Now You See It, Now You Don't: Heteroplasmy in Mitochondrial DNA," Satiable Curiosity, *Journal of Genetic Genealogy* 2 (2006): iv–v (http://www.jogg.info/21/SatiableCuriosity.pdf). "Heteroplasmy," *ISOGG Wiki* (http://www.isogg.org/wiki/Heteroplasmy).

[9] Athel Cornish-Bowden, "Nomenclature for Incompletely Specified Bases in Nucleic Acid Sequences: Recommendations 1984," *Nucleic Acids Research* 13, no. 9 (1985); archived at National Center for BioTechnology Information, *PubMed Central* (http://www.ncbi.nlm.nih.gov/pmc/articles/PMC341218/pdf/nar00303-0014.pdf).

[10] Behar et al., "A 'Copernican' Reassessment of the Human Mitochondrial DNA Tree from its Root." See also Mark Stoneking, "Hypervariable Sites in the mtDNA Control Region are Mutational Hotspots," *The American Journal of Human Genetics* 67, no. 4 (October 2000): 1029–32; accessed online (http://www.cell.com/ajhg/fulltext/S000292970763300X); DOI: http://dx.doi.org/10.1086/303092.

for analysis includes these locations. Due to the variability, more differences than expected may be seen if the locations are included.

Table 4. Heteroplasmy/nucleotide ambiguity codes[a]			
Symbol	Meaning	Symbol	Meaning
U	U (Uracil)	S	C or G
M	A or C	Y	C or T
R	A or G	K	G or T
W	A or T	V	A or C or G
H	A or C or T	B	C or G or T
D	A or G or T	X	G or A or T or C
N	G or A or T or C		

a. "How Do I Know if I Have an mtDNA (Mitochondrial DNA) Heteroplasmy? What is the Nomenclature?," Family Tree DNA, *Family Tree DNA Learning Center BETA* (https://www.familytreedna.com/learn/mtdna-testing/heteroplasmy-nomenclature/).

Match-List Thresholds

Family Tree DNA, one of the few companies offering mtDNA tests today, uses the thresholds shown in table 5 for comparisons and for reporting matches. The number of differences will be displayed as the genetic distance or as a number of steps difference between two test-takers. More than three mutations would rarely be seen in close matrilineal relationships, but it is not impossible, especially when one or more test-takers has a heteroplasmy.

Private or Family Mutations

Private or family mtDNA mutations are those that are not in hot spots and are not haplogroup-defining mutations. These mutations can be more recent and more genealogically relevant.

Distance to Most Recent Common Ancestor (MRCA)

It is difficult to predict the distance to the MRCA of two test-takers with an exact mtDNA match. An exact match can occur if the test-takers are siblings (with only one generation back to the MRCA, their mother) or more distantly related (for example, when the MRCA is an eighth great-grandmother born in the early 1700s). In some cases, incorporating mtDNA, atDNA, and strong documentary evidence may give the best chance of reaching a credible conclusion.

Table 5. Family Tree DNA match-list thresholds		
Test type	Match-list threshold	Comments
mtDNA (HVR1) low resolution test (no longer offered)	Exact matches in the same haplogroup	Exactly the same results for all markers compared (https://www.familytreedna.com/learn/faq-items/exact-match/); see also the "What is SmartMatching?" section (https://www.familytreedna.com/learn/user-guide/mtdna-myftdna/mt-matches-page/).
mtDNAPlus (HVR1 and HVR2) medium resolution test	Exact matches excluding 309 and 315	(https://www.familytreedna.com/learn/faq-items/exact-match/); see also "On the mtDNA-Matches Page, Are Only Exact Matches Shown?" section (https://www.familytreedna.com/learn/user-guide/mtdna-myftdna/mt-matches-page/). Locations 309 and 315 are excluded, as these frequently exhibit insertions or deletions.
mtFull (Full mtDNA sequence)	0–3 step matches including heteroplasmy, but excluding 309 and 315	

mtDNA Analysis

When using mtDNA to determine whether a matrilineal line descends from a biogeographical group, such as African or Native America, the haplogroup obtained from a low- or medium-resolution test can likely provide the answer. The *ISOGG Wiki* (http://www.isogg.org/wiki) and other online sources of information can be used to determine if the haplogroup is identified with a specific biogeographical-origin group.[11]

[11] "Human Mitochondrial DNA Haplogroup," *Wikipedia* (https://en.wikipedia.org/wiki/Human_mitochondrial_DNA_haplogroup); drill down to the haplogroup of interest by clicking on the links in the "Evolutionary relationship" section. Roberta Estes, "Native American Mitochondrial Haplogroups," *DNA-eXplained—Genetic Genealogy* (blog), 18 September 2013 (http://dna-explained.com/2013/09/18/native-american-mitochondrial-haplogroups/). Roberta Estes, "New Native Mitochondrial DNA Haplogroups Extrapolated from Anzick Match Results," *DNA-eXplained—Genetic Genealogy* (blog), 24 September 2014 (http://dna-explained.com/2014/09/24/new-mitochondrial-dna-haplogroups-extrapolated-from-anzick-match-results/). Estes summarizes research on Native American mtDNA haplogroups.

If the haplogroup is associated only with the specific group of interest, the matrilineal ancestor was part of that group. If the haplogroup contains members with more than one type of biogeographical origin, the matrilineal ancestor may be part of the group of interest or one of the other groups.

Mitochondrial DNA can be used to determine whether a test-taker is a descendant of one of two women—for example, two wives or mates of the same man. Analysis requires comparing the mtDNA test results from three (or more) test-takers:

- a descendant of woman number one
- a descendant of woman number two
- the person trying to determine which woman, if either, is the ancestor

If all three people test at the same level and have the same haplogroup assigned, there is a common matrilineal ancestor. The common ancestor could be recent or could be thousands of years back in time. This would be the result when the two focus women were sisters or matrilineal cousins. In this case the third test-taker cannot determine which woman is the ancestor. If the descendants of woman number one and woman number two are not in the same haplogroup, the one whose haplogroup matches the third test-taker (if any) shares an ancestor on the matrilineal line with the test-taker.

mtDNA Tools

James Lick's mtHap Haplogroup Analysis tool (http://dna.jameslick.com/mthap/) is useful to confirm a haplogroup provided by a testing company or to obtain an updated haplogroup if a company used an older version of the mtDNA haplotree.

Using a FASTA file as input, the mtHap tool compares the data to the rCRS, and outputs a report as shown in figure 6 that lists all differences between the FASTA data and the rCRS on HVR2 (positions 1 through 574), CR (positions 575 through 16000), and HVR1 (positions 16001 through 16569).

mtHap determines the haplogroup based on the FASTA file. The report header will indicate which *PhyloTree* build or haplotree version was used for the analysis. The tree used is sometimes a more recent version than that used by the testing company, causing a slightly different (usually more detailed) haplogroup to be indicated. For example, a testing company may list the mtDNA haplogroup as U5b1d1. Using the same FASTA data, mtHap lists the haplogroup that best matches the data as U5b1d1c—a more recently defined branch of the tree that is not yet part of the tree used by the testing company. Along with identifying the best haplogroup match, mtHap may also list several other "good" matches with less detailed haplogroup names (U5b1d1 and U5b1d, for example). The mtHap tool is usually updated soon after the release of a new *PhyloTree* build.

The report specifies, in numerical order and by region, the haplogroup's defining markers. It enumerates the marker path from the rCRS (haplogroup H2a2a1) to the haplogroup matching the FASTA data. Differences that are not part of the haplogroup definition are listed as "extras." These may be hot spots that were ignored in the analysis or private mutations. Other test-takers who share these same private mutations are likely more closely related to you than test-takers in the same haplogroup who do not have the private mutations.

Figure 6. Sample report from mtHap
Note that output from the mtHap tool is displayed in color on the website.
Various formatting options are used here to visually separate the output where color is used on the website.

mthap version 0.19a (2013-04-08); haplogroup data version PhyloTree Build 16 (2014-02-19)
raw data source sample.fasta (16KB)

FASTA format was uploaded. Based on the markers found, assuming the following regions were completely sequenced: HVR1 (16001~16569) HVR2 (1~574) CR (575~16000).

Found 16569 markers at 16569 positions covering 100.0% of mtDNA.

Markers found (shown as differences to rCRS):
HVR2: 73G 150T 263G (315.1C) 524.1A 524.2C
CR: 750G 1438G 2706G 3197C 4769G 5437T 5656G 7028T 7768G 7912A 8860G 9477A 11467G 11719A 12308G 12372A 13617C 14182C 14766T 15326G 15631G 15721C
HVR1: 16192T 16218T 16270T 16320T

Best mtDNA Haplogroup Matches:

1) U5b1d1c
Defining Markers for haplogroup U5b1d1c:
HVR2: 73G 150T 263G
CR: 750G 1438G 2706G 3197C 4769G 5437T 5656G 7028T 7768G 7912A 8860G 9477A 11467G 11719A 12308G 12372A 13617C 14182C 14766T 15326G 15631G 15721C
HVR1: 16192T 16218T 16270T 16320T

Marker path from rCRS to haplogroup U5b1d1c (plus extra markers):
H2a2a1(rCRS) ⇨ 263G ⇨ **H2a2a** ⇨ 8860G 15326G ⇨ **H2a2** ⇨ 750G ⇨ **H2a** ⇨ 4769G ⇨ **H2** ⇨ 1438G ⇨ **H** ⇨ 2706G 7028T ⇨ **HV** ⇨ 14766T ⇨ **R0** ⇨ 73G 11719A ⇨ **R** ⇨ 11467G 12308G 12372A ⇨ **U** ⇨ 16192T 16270T ⇨ **U5** ⇨ 3197C 9477A 13617C ⇨ **U5a'b** ⇨ 150T 7768G 14182C ⇨ **U5b** ⇨ 5656G ⇨ **U5b1** ⇨ 5437T ⇨ **U5b1d** ⇨ 15721C ⇨ **U5b1d1** ⇨ 7912A 15631G 16218T 16320T ⇨ **U5b1d1c** ⇨ *(315.1C) 524.1A 524.2C*

Good Match! Your results also had extra markers for this haplogroup:
Matches(29): 73G 150T 263G 750G 1438G 2706G 3197C 4769G 5437T 5656G 7028T 7768G 7912A 8860G 9477A 11467G 11719A 12308G 12372A 13617C 14182C 14766T 15326G 15631G 15721C 16192T 16218T 16270T 16320T
Extras(2): *(315.1C) 524.1A 524.2C*

MitoSearch (http://www.mitosearch.org/) offers some analysis tools and a comparison database for HVR1 and HVR2 mtDNA sequences. It is useful for entering mtDNA data, regardless of the testing company involved. If a person tested at a company that later went out of business or that no longer offers a comparison database, this may be the only way to find mtDNA matches.

Differences from the rCRS can be manually entered each time a search is performed, but it is more efficient to upload the data to the *MitoSearch* database. An ID number will be assigned and the data will be saved for future searches.

Table 6 shows results of a search for matches to user-ID 6UMUQ. They include User ID, a link to a pedigree (if available), haplogroup, HVR1 mutations (with the leading "16" missing, so that 192 indicates location 16192), number of differences (plus or minus) from the searcher's HVR1 mutation values, HVR2 mutations, and number of differences (plus or minus) from the searcher's HVR2 mutation values. The display may be filtered to show those who have entered only HVR1 values or those who have entered both HVR1 and HVR2 values.

Table 6. Sample search results from *MitoSearch*

Com-pare	User ID	Pedi-gree	Haplo-group	HVR1 Mutations	HVR1 Muta-tional Differ-ence	HVR2 Mutations	HVR2 Muta-tional Differ-ence
C	CG36E		U5	192T,218T,270T	−1	Not Tested	
C	29DNF		U5	192T,218T,270T, 320T	0	Not Tested	
C	SPE9C		U5	192T,218T,270T, 304C,320T	+1	Not Tested	
C	248RH		U5a	192T,218T,270T, 320T	0	073G,150T,263G, 315.1C,524.1C, 524.2A	0
C	6UMUQ		U5	192T,218T,270T, 320T	0	073G,150T,263G, 315.1C,524.1C, 524.2A	0

The values for user 6UMUQ are shown on the bottom row. Information about that user's matches indicate that

- user CG36E has tested only HVR1, is in haplogroup U5, shares three mutations with 6UMUQ, and has one missing mutation (320T);
- user 29DNF has tested only HVR1, is in haplogroup U5, shares four mutations with 6UMUQ, and has no missing or additional mutations not shared with 6UMUQ;
- user SPE9C has tested only HVR1, is in haplogroup U5, shares four mutations with 6UMUQ, and has one additional mutation (304C); and
- user 248RH has tested HVR1 and HVR2, is in haplogroup U5a (the detailed branch is known because more of the DNA was tested), shares the same four mutations with 6UMUQ in HVR1, shares the same six mutations with 6UMUQ in HVR2, and has no missing or additional mutations not shared with 6UMUQ.

---

[12] For example, when family legend indicates the matrilineal line is of Aleutian Islands descent and the mtDNA haplogroup is D2a1a, the DNA evidence is consistent with the family legend. See "Haplogroup D (mtDNA)," *Wikipedia* (https://en.wikipedia.org/wiki/Haplogroup_D_(mtDNA)).

[13] For example, clues can be gleaned if a close mtDNA match shows an ancestor in the same place at the same time as a tester's ancestor, the two test-takers share an mtDNA haplogroup, and there is documentary evidence indicating the ancestors could share a matrilineal line.

A group of test-takers of interest can be marked for comparison by clicking in the Compare column (indicated here with a "C" in column one) for each user of interest, then clicking "Compare" in the header. This enters the selected user-IDs into the Research Tools screen. Clicking the "Show" button on that window will display a list of HVR1 and HVR2 mutations for the selected IDs.

Clicking on any user-ID displays the mutational values along with details entered by that user, such as e-mail address, name, dates, origins, comments on the matrilineal line, and the most distant mtDNA ancestor. Researchers can contact each other to collaborate.

The ***mtDNAcommunity*** website (http://www.mtdnacommunity.org/) offers comparison tools that are similar to those on *MitoSearch*, but for use only on full mtDNA sequences.

Genetic Genealogy Kit (http://www.y-str.org/2014/07/genetic-genealogy-kit.html) can be downloaded and installed on one's own computer to analyze DNA for which one has access to a raw data (FASTA) file. The DNA data file remains on the computer. It is not transferred to an online database.

See "MtDNA Tools" on the *ISOGG Wiki* (http://www.isogg.org/wiki/MtDNA_tools) for information about additional tools.

Applications for mtDNA analysis

An mtDNA haplogroup can be used to determine
- whether a matrilineal line is of a specific ethnic or biogeographical ancestry;[12]
- whether two or more test-takers may be related or cannot be related through the matrilineal line; and
- clues about an ancestor's maiden name.[13]

Comparing two or more test-takers' mtDNA to a reference sequence can determine if those test-takers are in the same haplogroup and have few differences in their mtDNA test results. If so, they could be related through the matrilineal line. The common ancestor could be hundreds or thousands of years prior to the earliest documented matrilineal ancestor.

Chapter 4 Exercises

Use the family tree chart in Appendix A titled "Descendants of John Ira Jones and Mary Ann (Smith) Jones" to answer questions 1 through 3. The genealogist has confirmed that there are no common ancestors for the people named on the chart other than those shown. Each kinship link has been confirmed with strong documentary evidence.

Hint: The easiest way to answer these questions is to make a copy of the chart, then, beginning with Mary Ann Smith, mark all descendants who inherited her mtDNA. One at a time, move to women who married into the family and repeat the process, using a unique mark for each woman who contributed mtDNA to descendants.

In the following questions, a parenthesized number after an individual's name represents that person's number on the chart.

1. Which descendants shown inherited the mtDNA of Mary Ann (Smith) Jones (2)?

_____

_____

_____

2. Ira Gerball (20) died while serving in Vietnam. The military has located what is believed to be his body. To provide evidence that the correct body has been identified, the military is looking for family members to take an mtDNA test. Which people on the chart share the same mtDNA as Ira?

_____

_____

_____

3. Adoptee Angela Marks has used atDNA and documentary research to determine she may be a child of either Mandella Louise Smith (33) or Emmy Wick (34), both of whom are deceased and have no descendants shown on this chart. Both of Mandella's parents are deceased, but Emmy's parents are still living.

    a. If Emmy's parents (Max Wick (22) and Emmy Martin (28)) agree to take an mtDNA test, could the results help Angela determine whether Emmy Wick (34) or Mandella Louise Smith (33) may be her mother?

_____

_____

_____

b. What is the conclusion if Angela's mtDNA test matches both Max Wick (22) and Emmy Martin (28)? Would that double match be significant in a genealogically relevant timeframe?

_____

_____

_____

4. Susie Donelson and Josie McSpadden have taken full mtDNA sequence tests and are not shown on each other's list of matches. The chart below shows their mtDNA results as compared to the rCRS as well as outlines of their well-researched matrilineal lines.

	Susie Donelson mtDNA Haplogroup U5b1d1	Josie McSpadden mtDNA Haplogroup U5b1d1
HVR2		263G
CR	15607R	8542Y
HVR1	16192T	
mtDNA Line:	Tempy Gordy Sarah (Gordy) Parker Elizabeth (Parker) Richards Bonnie (Richards) Carter Mary (Carter) Vick Janice (Vick) Martin Vickie (Martin) Donelson Susie Donelson	Possibly Tempy Gordy (Speculative Link) Elizabeth (unknown) Rogers Sarah (Rogers) Bell Annie May (Bell) Kelly Martha (Kelly) Patrick Dicey (Kelly) McSpadden Josie McSpadden

a. Do the test results prove they are not related on the matrilineal line? Why or why not?

_____

_____

_____

b. Could other kinds of DNA tests help answer this question more definitively?

_____

_____

_____

5. Annabell Martin was told her fifth great-grandmother was a Cherokee who left the reservation to marry Annabell's fifth great-grandfather. Which of the following must be true for an mtDNA test to help Annabell prove this story? Mark all that apply.

    a. There must be a direct matrilineal line from the fifth great-grandmother to Annabell.

    b. There must be a direct matrilineal line from the fifth great-grandmother to any living descendant in the line who is willing to take a test.

    c. A full mtDNA sequence test must be used, as this provides the most conclusive evidence.

    d. A low- or medium-resolution mtDNA test should be sufficient, as the haplogroup alone is generally enough to identify Native American ancestry.

    e. At least three test-takers will be needed for conclusive proof.

_____

_____

_____

6. Two test-takers who suspect a common ancestor on the matrilineal line take medium-resolution mtDNA tests (HVR1 and HVR2). Neither appears on the match list of the other. The thoroughly researched and well-documented matrilineal lines, with known dates and places, are shown below.

Sarah's mtDNA Line	Jane's mtDNA Line
Jane (Vick) Otis, b. 1800 Rowan County, North Carolina; d. 1870 Copiah County, Mississippi	
Mary Otis, b. 1825 Rowan County, North Carolina; d. 1900 Angelina County, Texas	Elizabeth Otis, b. unknown date and place; m. 1845 Rowan County, North Carolina
Emma Ryan, b. 1860 Angelina County, Texas; d. 1940 Dallas, Texas	Martha Parrott, b. 1858 Conecuh County, Alabama; d. 1930 Conecuh County, Alabama
Joyce Johnson, b. 1890 Angelina County, Texas; d. 1960 Dallas, Texas	Dollie Richards, b. 1888 Conecuh County, Alabama; d. 1940 Conecuh County, Alabama
Sarah Richards, b. 1916 Dallas, Texas	Bonnie Jackson, b. 1920 Conecuh County, Alabama; d. 1970 Yell County, Arkansas
	Jane Smith, b. 1940 Yell County, Arkansas

a. Does the fact that these two test-takers are not on each other's match list preclude Jane (Vick) Otis from being the mother of both Mary Otis and Elizabeth Otis?

_____

_____

_____

b. Would it be advantageous for Sarah and Jane to upgrade to a full mtDNA sequence test?

_____

_____

_____

c. What other things might be considered based on the lineages shown?

_____

_____

_____

7. Sarah and Jane upgrade to full mtDNA sequence tests and receive the results below. Neither appears on the match list of the other.

Sarah's full mtDNA sequence test results	
Haplogroup	U5b1d1c
HVR1 differences from rCRS	16192T, 16218T, 16270T, 16320T
HVR2 differences from rCRS	73G, 150T, 263G, 315.1C, 523.1C. 523.2A
Coding Region differences from rCRS	750G, 1438G, 2706G, 3197C, 4769G, 5437T, 5656G, 7028T, 7768G, 7912A, 8860G, **9138Y**, 9477A, 11476G, 11719A, 12308G, 12372A, 13617C, 14182C, 14766T, 14326G, 15631G, 15721C

Jane's full mtDNA sequence test results	
Haplogroup	U5b1d1c
HVR1 differences from rCRS	16192T, **16193R**, 16218T, 16270T, 16320T
HVR2 differences from rCRS	73G, 150T, 263G, 315.1C, 523.1C. 523.2A
Coding Region differences from rCRS	750G, 1438G, 2706G, 3197C, 4769G, 5437T, 5656G, **6260R**, 7028T, 7768G, 7912A, 8860G, 9477A, 11476G, 11719A, 12308G, 12372A, 13617C, 14182C, 14766T, 14326G, 15326G, 15631G, 15721C

a. Does the fact that these two test-takers are not on each other's match list preclude Jane (Vick) Otis from being the mother of both Mary Otis and Elizabeth Otis? Do these results prove Jane is the mother of Mary and Elizabeth?

_____

_____

_____

b. Do these results explain why neither appears on the match list of the other?

_____

_____

_____

c. What do the Ys and Rs in the list of mtDNA differences (shown in bold above) from the reference sequence mean?

_____

_____

_____

Genealogical Applications for atDNA

What is atDNA?

Autosomal DNA (atDNA) consists of the twenty-two pairs of non-sex chromosomes found within the nucleus of every cell. The twenty-two autosomes, or autosomal DNA chromosomes, are numbered approximately in relation to their sizes, with autosome 1 being the largest and autosome 22 being the smallest.

While a mother's egg is being formed, her chromosome pairs can exchange DNA during recombination, which is discussed below. As a result, the chromosomes in the egg are a random mixture of the mother's parents' DNA. The egg contains one copy of each autosomal chromosome, which could be called the maternal chromosome. No two eggs will have the same DNA.

Recombination also occurs during formation of a father's sperm, so that a sperm cell contains a random mixture of the father's parents' DNA. The sperm contains one copy of each autosomal chromosome, which could be called the paternal chromosome. No two sperm cells will have the same DNA.

When the sperm fertilizes the egg, the maternal and paternal chromosomes form a full set of atDNA in the nucleus of the cell. The DNA of the child, therefore, is a random mixture of the DNA of the four grandparents. Non-identical siblings inherit random mixtures of the DNA of the four grandparents.

atDNA Inheritance Patterns

Since a child's genome is the same size as each of his parents' genomes, a child can inherit only 50 percent of each parent's total DNA. Beyond the parents, a child will inherit a variable amount of DNA from each individual in a given generation. For example, a child receives an average of 25 percent of his or her DNA from each of the four grandparents. When comparing a child's DNA to that of each individual grandparent, the percent shared can range considerably, but the average is always 25 percent. See the example in table 1.

Table 1. Percentage of DNA shared by grandchildren and grandparents

Grandchild	Paternal Grandfather	Paternal Grandmother	Maternal Grandfather	Maternal Grandmother	Average
Expected:	25.0	25.0	25.0	25.0	25.0
April	21.2	28.8	23.4	26.6	25.0
Hiram	20.5	29.5	28.6	21.4	25.0
Corey	30.1	19.9	24.6	25.4	25.0
Samantha	25.5	24.5	18.9	31.1	25.0

Table 2. Average percentage of DNA received from each ancestor in specific generations

Generation	Average percentage of DNA received from ancestors in that generation
Parents	50.0
Grandparents	25.0
G-Grandparents	12.5
2G-Grandparents	6.25
3G-Grandparents	3.125
4G-Grandparents	1.563
5G-Grandparents	0.781

At some point, people no longer receive DNA from *every* ancestor in a generation. Current analysis estimates that around the seventh generation, plus or minus two, people no longer inherit DNA from every ancestor, but from only a subset of the ancestors in that generation.[1] This divergence means that individuals have both a genealogical family tree and a genetic family tree. The genealogical family tree contains the name of every genealogical ancestor—every person who had offspring that ultimately led to an individual. In contrast, a person's genetic family tree contains only the names of those ancestors who provided a piece of the DNA that the person carries. The genetic family tree is a very small subset of the genealogical family tree. Siblings have different genetic

---

[1] Graham Coop, "How Many Genetic Ancestors Do I Have?," The Coop Lab, Population and Evolutionary Genetics, UC Davis, *gcbias*, 11 November 2013 (https://gcbias.org/2013/11/11/how-does-your-number-of-genetic-ancestors-grow-back-over-time/).

family trees, even though they have an identical genealogical family tree. Only identical twins share a genetic family tree.

Figure 1 shows an example of a fictional genetic family tree, where ancestors who have provided DNA to the terminal descendant are shaded. The unshaded ancestors are not genetic ancestors, although they are genealogical ancestors.

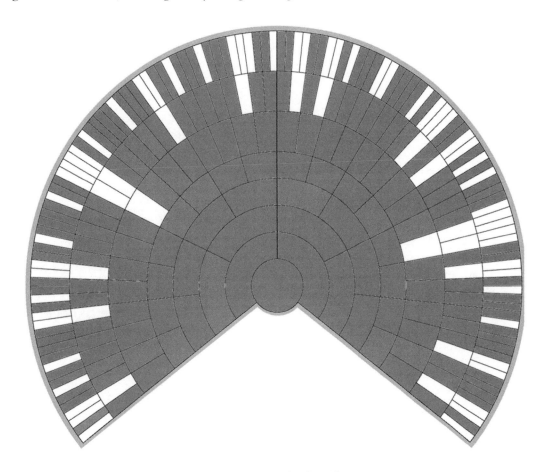

Figure 1. Genetic family tree

The fact that genealogical trees and genetic trees differ has significant implications for atDNA analysis and interpretation. For example, two descendants of the same person will not share DNA and will not be identified as genetic matches unless that common ancestor is found in the genetic family tree of both descendants. Similarly, if a particular ethnicity is found in an ancestor who is in a person's genealogical family tree but not in the genetic family tree, that ethnicity will not be detected in that person's atDNA.

Recombination

When a mother forms an egg cell, the DNA undergoes a process called recombination, in which the mother's paternal and maternal chromosomes exchange DNA. The same process takes place when a father forms a sperm cell. During meiosis—a cell division that creates eggs and sperm for reproduction—the cell copies each of the twenty-two pairs of chromosomes so that there are a total of eighty-eight autosomes (twenty-two pairs of autosomes (a total of forty-four), doubled, for a total of eighty-eight). For example, during meiosis a single egg- or sperm-precursor cell will contain four copies of chromosome 1—two identical copies of the maternal chromosome and two identical copies of the paternal chromosome.

Figure 2 shows the duplication of chromosome 1 in a mother's egg-precursor cell or father's sperm-precursor cell. There will be four copies of the chromosome after duplication. The two copies of the maternal chromosome (in white in figure 2) are called sister chromosomes, meaning that they are identical copies created by the duplication of a single chromosome. Similarly, the two copies of the paternal chromosome (shaded gray in figure 2) are also called sister chromosomes.

In contrast, a copy of the maternal chromosome is called a non-sister chromosome when compared to a copy of the paternal chromosome.

Recombination can occur between *any* of the four copies. If recombination occurs between one of the copies of the maternal chromosome and one of the copies of the paternal chromosome, a detectable crossover-event occurs, as shown in figure 3.

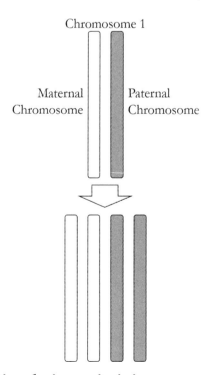

Chromosome 1

Maternal
Chromosome

Paternal
Chromosome

Figure 2. DNA duplication during meiosis in an egg- or sperm-precursor cell

Although some recombination must occur during meiosis in order for there to be a viable sperm or egg cell, there is no requirement that all chromosomes undergo recombination. It is not unusual for a parent to pass down entire unchanged chromosomes to the next generation. In that case, the child will receive an exact copy of a single grandparent's chromosome.

After recombination is complete, the four copies of each chromosome are segregated into four separate cells. One of these cells becomes the egg or sperm that passes down the chromosome to the next generation. This results in a total of twenty-two autosomes and one sex chromosome being packaged into each egg and sperm.

In figure 3, for example, the sperm or egg cell may receive any of the four chromosomes, including one of the two chromosomes that have undergone recombination or one of the two chromosomes that have not undergone recombination.

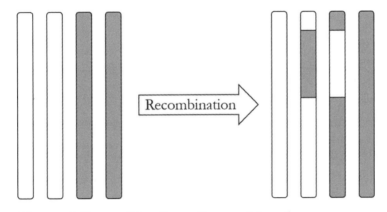

Figure 3. Recombination of non-sister chromosomes

Women tend to have more recombination events than men. According to one recent study, the twenty-two chromosomes that a woman passed to the next generation in an egg cell experienced an average of approximately forty-two recombination events, while the twenty-two chromosomes that a man passed to the next generation in a sperm cell experienced an average of only twenty-seven recombination events.[2] Of course, this will vary considerably from person to person.

Figure 4 shows the recombination that occurred in a mother and father for the first five chromosomes. A graph like this is created by comparing an individual to all four grandparents. The top row is the individual's paternal chromosome, showing where recombination occurred in the father between the paternal grandparents' chromosomes. The bottom row is the maternal chromosome, showing where recombination occurred in the mother between the maternal grandparents' chromosomes.

---

[2] Reshmi Chowdhury et al., "Genetic Analysis of Variation in Human Meiotic Recombination," *PLOS Genetics*, 18 September 2009; accessed online
(http://journals.plos.org/plosgenetics/article?id=10.1371/journal.pgen.1000648); DOI:
10.1371/journal.pgen.1000648.

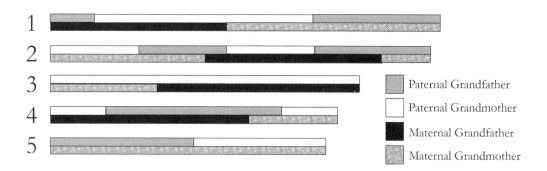

Figure 4. Example of recombination of the first five chromosomes

As shown in figure 4, recombination will vary. The maternal copy of chromosome 5, obtained from the mother's egg, did not undergo recombination and thus the child has an exact copy of the maternal grandmother's chromosome. In contrast, the paternal copy of chromosome 2, obtained from the father's sperm, experienced three different recombination events.

With each generation, shared DNA segments tend to get smaller because of recombination, although it is possible for a segment to be randomly passed down for generations without being affected.[3]

The locations of the recombination-crossover events for each test-taker determine the start and stop points of shared or overlapping segments. Each descendant may have different crossover points, causing segments to vary in size with some or all cousins who share an overlapping segment. Analysis of these segments is covered in more detail below.

Finding and Classifying Genetic Matches

Due to recombination and the fact that we inherit only half of each parent's DNA, it is possible to estimate, on average, how much DNA two genetic relatives should share. Table 3 correlates relationship with the amount of shared DNA, stated in percentages and centimorgans (cM). A cM is a measurement of the genetic distance between two points on a chromosome, using the frequency of recombination between those two points as the measuring stick. One cM is equivalent to a 1 percent chance of a recombination event occurring somewhere between these two points in a single generation. The number of base pairs to which a cM corresponds varies widely across the genome, and varies by gender, but on average one cM corresponds to approximately one million base pairs.

Since recombination is random, actual amounts of shared DNA will vary from the expected averages. The numbers in table 3 are based on the tests most commonly used today, which cover approximately 6800 cM of atDNA.

---

[3] Steve Mount, "Genetic Genealogy and the Single Segment," *On Genetics*, 19 February 2011 (http://on-genetics.blogspot.com/2011/02/genetic-genealogy-and-single-segment.html).

Table 3. Average amount of DNA shared in various relationships

Relationship	Percentage of DNA shared	Centimorgans (cM) of DNA shared
Parent/child	50	3400.00
Full siblings	50	2550.00
Grandparent/grandchild, aunt/uncle/niece/nephew, half sibling	25	1700.00
Great-grandparent/great-grandchild, first cousins, great-aunt/uncle/niece/nephew, half aunt/uncle/niece/nephew	12.5	850.00
First cousins once removed, half first cousins, great granduncle/grandaunt	6.25	425.00
Second cousins, first cousins twice removed	3.125	212.50
Second cousins once removed, half second cousins	1.563	106.25
Third cousins, second cousins twice removed	0.781	53.13
Third cousins once removed	0.391	26.56
Fourth cousins	0.195	13.28

Table 3 demonstrates that the amount of DNA we receive from our ancestors decreases with every generation. The same is true for genealogical cousins; at every generation, the likelihood decreases that a person shares a segment of DNA with a genealogical cousin. For genealogical cousins to share DNA, they both must inherit the same or an overlapping segment of DNA from the common ancestor.

Table 4 shows estimates from each of the major genetic genealogy testing companies of the likelihood that genealogical relatives will share a detectable amount of DNA. A detectable amount of DNA is any amount above the company's comparison threshold (discussed below).

The numbers presented in tables 3 and 4 will typically be greater when comparing individuals from an endogamous population. Endogamy is the practice of individuals marrying within the same group over a long period of time, resulting in test-takers having multiple common ancestral couples. In this case, the population will have lower levels of genetic diversity and individuals within the population will tend to share more DNA. Relationship predictions will be skewed toward closer relationships because relationship-predicting algorithms typically assume two test-takers share only one ancestral couple. Examples of endogamous populations are Acadians, the Amish, Ashkenazi Jews, people from Newfoundland, island groups, and people from many small towns and rural areas in pre-twentieth-century America. Test-takers with ancestry from these regions will have a large number of matches at the testing company and should be cautious about the accuracy of the company's relationship predictions.

Table 4. Likelihood of detectable amounts of shared DNA with a genealogical relative (%)

Relationship	23andMe[4]	AncestryDNA[5]	Family Tree DNA[6]
Closer than second cousin	100	100	>99
Second cousin	>99	100	>99
Third cousin	~90	98	>90
Fourth cousin	~45	71	>50
Fifth cousin	~15	32	>10
Sixth cousin or greater	<5	<11	<2

Each of the major genetic-genealogy testing companies provides a list of individuals in the company's database who share DNA with the test-taker above a predetermined threshold. This threshold, which is slightly different at each company, is an attempt to eliminate false-positive matches while identifying as many true matches as possible.

A false-positive match is any shared DNA segment that does not result from sharing a recent common ancestor. A false-positive match between two individuals can occur for a variety of reasons. For example, a false-positive match can occur because the DNA is not separated into the maternal and paternal chromosomes before it is compared; they can also occur because of random mutations that result in matching between two individuals. Although the exact percentage of false positives is not known, it is generally accepted within the community that a significant percentage of small segments of 5 cM and less are false positives.

As discussed below, in addition to cM lengths, the minimum threshold of several of the testing companies use SNP density as a factor. Every shared segment of DNA contains a series of SNPs analyzed by the testing company. The density of the SNPs in that segment can be important when determining whether a segment is truly shared by two people or whether it is a false positive, especially when the segment is small. For

---

[4] "The Probability of Detecting Different Types of Cousins," 23andMe, *23andMe Customer Care* (https://customercare.23andme.com/hc/en-us/articles/202907230-The-probability-of-detecting-different-types-of-cousins).

[5] "Should Other Family Members Get Tested?," *AncestryDNA* (http://dna.ancestry.com/insights/2892A529-4765-4E7E-9588-170CC90DBFC8); page available for registered users.

[6] "What is the Probability That My Relative and I Share Enough DNA for Family Finder to Detect?," Family Tree DNA, *Family Tree DNA Learning Center BETA* (https://www.familytreedna.com/learn/autosomal-ancestry/universal-dna-matching/probability-relative-share-enough-dna-family-finder-detect/).

example, for a 5 cM segment with only 50 tested SNPs the likelihood that the sharing could be random is much greater than for a 5 cM segment with 500 tested SNPs. At much greater cM lengths, however, the SNP density can be less of a concern, as the overall number of SNPs will be very large and the likelihood of the segment being a false positive is much lower.

Reporting Genetic Matching by the atDNA Testing Companies

There are currently three major atDNA testing companies: 23andMe (http://www.23andme.com/), AncestryDNA (http://dna.ancestry.com/), and Family Tree DNA (http://www.familytreedna.com/). After the testing company receives a saliva or cheek swab sample from the test-taker, the DNA in that sample is extracted and compared to the DNA of every other test-taker in the company's database. This identifies people in the database who share one or more segments of the test-taker's DNA. The results of the comparison are presented as a list of genetic matches ranked in order from the match who shares the most DNA to the match who shares the least DNA.

The ways in which testing companies report matches vary slightly. Below are details about interpreting the list of genetic matches provided by each of the testing companies.

23andMe
The list of genetic matches at 23andMe is called "DNA Relatives." DNA Relatives[7] is an opt-in feature, so a test-taker will not see all of the identified genetic relatives. The company imposes a limit on the size of the list, currently around two thousand matches. For relatives that do opt-in, the display will show a username (an actual name, initials, or a combination of the two), Y-DNA (when the match is male) and mtDNA haplogroups of matches, and surnames or other information that have been entered into the match's profile.

Some test-takers at 23andMe opt for "Open Sharing," meaning that their name, overlapping DNA segments, and ancestry reports (Ancestry Composition and Neanderthal Ancestry) are available. For matches who haven't opted into Open Sharing, an individual sharing-connection will have to be formed. A test-taker has two options for sharing information with a match. The test-taker can share just his name and profile, or the test-taker can share his name and profile and extend an invitation to exchange information about shared DNA segments. The match has the option to ignore, accept, or deny the sharing invitation.

There are several different matching thresholds used by 23andMe. For atDNA, the threshold is 7 cM and at least 700 SNPs for the first segment of DNA, and then 5 cM and 700 SNPs for each additional segment. For matches that share atDNA in a region on both the maternal and paternal chromosomes—called a *fully identical region* (FIR)—the matching threshold is lowered to 5 cM and 500 SNPs.

---

[7] "DNA Relatives: How It Works," 23andMe, *23andMe Customer Care* (https://customercare.23andme.com/hc/en-us/articles/202907200-DNA-Relatives-How-it-works); Path: Customer Care > Tools > DNA Relatives.

For X-DNA, discussed in a later chapter, the threshold depends on the gender of the two individuals in the analysis, as males have only one X chromosome. For a male-to-male comparison, the threshold is 1 cM and 200 SNPs. For a male-to-female comparison, the threshold is 6 cM and 600 SNPs. For a female-to-female comparison, the threshold is 6 cM and 1200 SNPs. Notably, the DNA Relatives list at 23andMe may include matches who share only X-DNA.

AncestryDNA

Genetic matches at AncestryDNA are called "DNA Matches." As with other genetic genealogy testing companies, results are listed based on total shared DNA. Individuals sharing the most DNA with the test-taker are shown first. For each match, a predicted relationship and a possible relationship range is provided. Test-takers can also see the total amount of DNA they share with each genetic match. Matches are identified by real name or Ancestry username; they can be contacted only through the Ancestry interface. Matches may optionally link their results to family trees and permit public access to the trees. Trees are displayed on the matches' profile pages.

To eliminate some false-positive matches, AncestryDNA utilizes an algorithm (currently called Underdog) to phase a test-taker's raw data prior to searching for genetic matches in the database. Phasing is a process by which the test-taker's raw data are segregated to categorize alleles that were inherited from the maternal and paternal chromosomes.

AncestryDNA also applies an algorithm (currently called Timber) that identifies segments of DNA called "pile-up" regions, which appear to be shared by hundreds or thousands of people rather than just among close relatives. These segments are characterized by AncestryDNA as being inherited from a distant ancestor outside a genealogically relevant timeframe; they are not utilized for matching.[8] For the remaining segments, the matching threshold at AncestryDNA is 5 cM.

Family Tree DNA

Genetic matches identified by Family Tree DNA are called "Matches." Test-takers are provided with their matches' usernames, e-mail addresses, relationship range predictions, Y-DNA (when male) and mtDNA haplogroups (if they've taken these tests), total shared amount of atDNA, and the longest segment of shared atDNA. Each match's surnames of interest will be available if entered into the profile, and Family Tree DNA will identify surnames in common between the test-taker and the match. Family Tree DNA also provides a family-tree interface that allows review of a match's tree, if the match has made one available.

Family Tree DNA's matching threshold was updated in mid-2016. Following the update, test-takers are always identified as a match if they share at least one segment of at least 9 cM. If the longest segment shared by two test-takers is between 7.69 cM and 9 cM, they

---

[8] Catherine A. Ball et al., "Ancestry DNA Matching White Paper: Discovering IBD Matches Across a Large, Growing Database," *AncestryDNA* (http://dna.ancestry.com/resource/whitePaper/AncestryDNA-Matching-White-Paper.pdf). Anne Swayne, "Behind The New AncestryDNA Feature: Amount of Shared DNA," *Tech Roots*, 6 January 2016 (http://blogs.ancestry.com/techroots/behind-the-new-ancestrydna-feature-amount-of-shared-dna/).

will be identified as a match only if they share a total of 20 cM. If the longest segment shared by two test-takers is less than 7.69 cM, they will not be identified as a match. There is a separate formula for people with Ashkenazi heritage, but the formula is proprietary. [9]

Family Tree DNA also reports shared X-DNA. The threshold for X-DNA matching is 1 cM and 500 SNPs, although matches are not identified based on sharing X-DNA alone. A match must share atDNA above the threshold before X-DNA sharing is reported.[10]

atDNA Tools for Genealogists

Each of the three testing companies provides tools to assist in identifying the common ancestry with a match, which is the primary goal of most genetic genealogy analysis. These tools vary greatly from company to company. Provided below are details about some of the most popular tools offered by the testing companies.

23andMe

At 23andMe, the "Compare DNA" tool (reached by clicking on "Tools," then "DNA Relatives," then "DNA") provides data—chromosome number, start and stop locations, total shared cM, and total number of SNPs—for every segment of DNA shared by the test-taker and any match who has (1) opted in to DNA Relatives, and (2) agreed to share genomes with the test-taker. The tool maps the shared segments to a chromosome browser, which is a visual reproduction of the twenty-two autosomes and the X chromosome. Shared segment information can alternatively be viewed in a table or can be downloaded into a spreadsheet.

Although 23andMe originally offered many more tools, the company completely overhauled the service in 2016 and now offers fewer options for analysis.

AncestryDNA

AncestryDNA offers a suite of tools. For example, for every match the test-taker can see the total amount of shared DNA and the number of shared segments, although AncestryDNA does not identify the chromosome or the start- and stop-points.

The "Shared Matches" tool, available for each of the test-taker's matches, identifies everyone in the database who has been identified as a cousin to both the test-taker and the selected match—but only when that cousin is predicted to be a fourth cousin or closer to the test-taker. For example, to use the Shared Matches tool the test-taker first selects a match called Julie. Clicking on the Shared Matches tab in Julie's profile will show every match at a fourth cousin or closer relationship to the test-taker who is shared by the test-taker and Julie. They may share many more cousins beyond the fourth cousin range, but these are not currently shown by AncestryDNA.

---

[9] Blaine T. Bettinger, "Family Tree DNA Updates Matching Thresholds," *The Genetic Genealogist*, 24 May 2016 (http://thegeneticgenealogist.com/2016/05/24/family-tree-dna-updates-matching-thresholds/).

[10] "Does the Family Finder test use X-chromosome DNA (X-DNA) test results?," Family Tree DNA, *Family Tree DNA Learning Center BETA* (https://www.familytreedna.com/learn/autosomal-ancestry/universal-dna-matching/use-x-dna-test-results/).

In addition to Shared Matches, AncestryDNA provides a "Shared Ancestor Hint" tool that compares family trees belonging to the test-taker and a match to identify shared ancestors. The tool considers a variety of factors, including the completeness of the trees, the similarity of the ancestor in the two trees, and the number of ancestors shared by the test-taker and the match. Although the tool alone does not establish that the shared DNA came from the identified ancestor or ancestors, it is a clue that the test-taker and match can pursue.

"DNA Circles" is another tool offered by AncestryDNA. A DNA Circle is a group of individuals identified as having the same ancestor in their family trees and who share one or more segments of DNA with at least one other individual in the circle, thereby forming a genetic network. See figure 5, where solid lines (between members of a family group) and dashed lines (between family groups) indicate shared segments of DNA. Test-takers can only have a DNA Circle if a public tree is linked to their DNA-test results. A DNA Circle can be formed when there is a minimum of three different family groups, each consisting of one or more descendants related no closer than the level of first cousin once removed. A DNA Circle would not form for an ancestral couple who only has grandchildren, as those descendants would all have a genealogical relationship of first cousin or closer. DNA Circles are not fixed and can change due to the actions of just a single individual within the circle. For example, when a member of the circle removes the shared ancestor from their tree or makes an edit to that shared ancestor, that action can introduce enough uncertainty that AncestryDNA's algorithm will dismantle the entire DNA Circle. A DNA Circle is not proof that all members of the circle inherited the shared segments of DNA from the identified ancestor. It should only be considered a clue for additional research.[11]

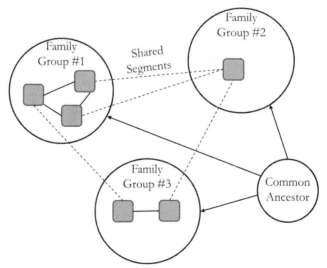

A family group is anyone first cousin once removed or closer

Figure 5. A genetic network created with DNA Circles at AncestryDNA

[11] Anne Swayne, "Exploring Your DNA Circles," *AncestryDNA* (http://c.ancestry.com/cs/media/exploring-your-dna-circles.pdf).

In contrast to DNA Circles, which creates the circle based on shared DNA and shared ancestors in public family trees, the "New Ancestor Discoveries" tool at AncestryDNA identifies potential new ancestors and relatives using only DNA. A New Ancestor Discovery is revealed when the test-taker shares significant amounts of DNA with multiple members of an existing DNA Circle, as shown in figure 6. A New Ancestor Discovery is not proof that the test-taker is a descendant of that ancestor. Instead, a test-taker is predicted by AncestryDNA to be a descendant of the identified ancestor in approximately 50 percent of New Ancestor Discoveries, while in 30 percent of the cases the test-taker shares multiple common ancestors with other members of the group. In the remaining 20 percent the test-taker is a collateral-line relative to the other group members. As with Shared Matches and DNA Circles, New Ancestor Discoveries are hints that can be pursued.

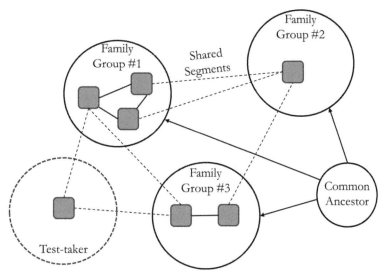

A family group is anyone first cousin once removed or closer

Figure 6. A genetic network created with New Ancestor Discoveries tool at AncestryDNA

Family Tree DNA

Family Tree DNA also offers an array of tools for analyzing genetic connections. For example, the company offers two tools for examining the interrelatedness of genetic matches, the "In Common With" tool and the "Matrix" tool. The In Common With (ICW) tool is accessed by clicking a double-arrow icon next to a match's username. The tool shows all genetic matches shared by the test-taker and the selected match.

The Matrix tool, located on the Family Finder Dashboard, is similar to the ICW tool. Matrix reveals whether two matches share DNA. It can compare up to ten matches at a time, selected by the test-taker. A grid format is used to compare the selected matches

---

[12] For example, when family legend indicates the matrilineal line is of Aleutian Islands descent and the mtDNA haplogroup is D2a1a, the DNA evidence is consistent with the family legend. See "Haplogroup D (mtDNA)," *Wikipedia* (https://en.wikipedia.org/wiki/Haplogroup_D_(mtDNA)).

to one another. If two matches share DNA, their intersecting cell on the grid will be highlighted and checked, otherwise the cell will be blank.

Neither the ICW tool nor the Matrix tool determines whether the same segment of DNA is shared by all matches under study. For example, although the Matrix tool reveals that (1) the test-taker and match 1 share DNA; (2) the test-taker and match 2 share DNA; and (3) match 1 and match 2 share DNA, there is no guarantee that all three people share the same segment. There is consensus among genetic genealogists that, in a high percentage of cases, in-common-with status represents sharing of at least the same segment among three or more members of the group, but the actual percentage is unknown.

Similar to 23andMe, Family Tree DNA also offers a "Chromosome Browser" tool. Unlike 23andMe, Family Tree DNA's tool is available for every genetic match identified by the company. Up to five people at a time can be compared to the test-taker. Segment data from the chromosome browser analysis can be reviewed in a visual display or a table, or downloaded to a spreadsheet. Family Tree DNA also offers the option to download segment data for all matches into a single spreadsheet.

Third-Party Tools
Third-party tools offer analysis that is not possible with testing companies' tools. One of the primary benefits of third-party tools is the ability to compare test results from different companies. This cross-company comparison is only possible using these third-party tools.

Test-takers must upload their raw data from the testing company to the third-party site in order to use tools at the site. Comparisons can only be made with other test-takers who have uploaded their test results.

The largest and most well-known third-party site is *GEDmatch* (http://www.gedmatch.com). *GEDmatch* was originally created to enable genealogists to compare DNA test results and GEDCOM files to facilitate identification of common ancestors among two or more genetic matches.[12] *GEDmatch* has continued to grow in the ensuing years. Its database now has hundreds of thousands of profiles, and stored GEDCOM files hold millions of pieces of data.

Among the many powerful tools at *GEDmatch* is "One-to-Many," which compares a test-taker's DNA to all others in the database and identifies genetic cousins (ranked by the total amount of shared DNA). This is the same function performed by the testing companies, but *GEDmatch* offers several advantages. In addition to comparing results from multiple companies, the One-to-Many tool provides genealogists with the ability to adjust the matching threshold. The default *GEDmatch* threshold is 7 cM, but it can be raised or lowered based on the user's goals.

GEDmatch also offers a "One-to-One" tool, which compares the DNA of two individuals in the database and reports the results in either a table or chromosome-browser form. In addition, *GEDmatch* offers an array of different admixture (that is, ethnicity)

---

[12] GEDCOM, which stands for Genealogical Data Communication, is a standardized format for packaging electronic genealogical data, usually a family tree.

calculators, each with different reference populations. Users have the option of viewing the results of the admixture calculators by percentage or in a chromosome browser showing where along the chromosomes the ethnicity predictions are made. Additional tools are available from this third-party site, and more are continually being developed.

One of the main advantages of *GEDmatch* is the ability to directly compare relatives' DNA. At the testing companies, a test-taker can compare his or her own DNA to all matches, but the only way to compare the DNA of two relatives to each other is with an ICW tool—and those tools do not identify the shared segment. At *GEDmatch*, users can choose to run tools and analysis either on their own DNA results or on results belonging to a genetic match (once the match's kit number is known). This gives users the ability to directly compare two or more matches to one another using the One-to-One tool.

Another popular third-party site is *DNAGedcom* (http://www.dnagedcom.com), which helps genetic genealogists compile and analyze their testing data. The tool allows users to download specific data from 23andMe, AncestryDNA, and Family Tree DNA. The data that can be downloaded varies for each of the companies, but for Family Tree DNA, for example, it includes lists of all genetic matches, all shared segments from the chromosome browser, and all ICW combinations. This downloaded information is stored on *DNAGedcom's* servers for analysis by tools housed there. Segment organizational tools JWorks and KWorks arrange segments of DNA by chromosome and start location, and group together overlapping segments. While not confirmed triangulation groups[13]—since it is unknown whether a group of overlapping segments are shared by all matches without more information—this is a helpful organizational tool. *DNAGedcom* also hosts the "Autosomal DNA Segment Analyzer" (ADSA), a tool developed for visually aligning shared segments of DNA without using a spreadsheet.

There are several other third-party tools, with more being developed all the time. Genetic genealogists must stay current with the latest tools. Before using any third-party tools, the site's privacy policy should be examined to determine whether the test-taker agrees to the ways in which data will be made available to other users.

Test Strategies for atDNA

Autosomal DNA can be a powerful tool for confirming or rejecting a genealogical hypothesis, including even the most well-established genealogies supported by years' worth of documentary evidence. Determining who to test (other than oneself) to examine a genealogical hypothesis can be challenging. The decision requires knowledge about the genealogical question at hand and about the limitations of atDNA. For example, atDNA may not be the best tool to examine a hypothesis surrounding a man who lived four hundred years ago. Due to the random inheritance of atDNA there is no guarantee that genealogical relatives more distant than second cousins will share detectable

---

[13] A triangulation group consists of three or more test-takers who match one another on the same or an overlapping segment of a particular chromosome. Because we have one copy of each chromosome from our mother and one from our father, two triangulated groups can exist for each segment of each chromosome.

amounts of DNA. Results showing that two people do not share DNA is typically not helpful evidence beyond the second cousin relationship, and there will often be a need to compare the atDNA of multiple individuals.

In most instances a two-pronged approach can be used to confirm or reject a genealogical hypothesis. First, it is possible to "fish" for genetic matches who may be related to or descended from the individuals involved in the genealogical hypothesis by simply taking an atDNA test at one or more of the testing companies. This will place the test-taker's DNA record in the testing-company database where it will be compared to every test result. Second, it is possible to do targeted testing of relatives or other individuals to more directly find the DNA of interest. If a research project involves ancestor Hugh Stone, it may be beneficial to not only test and look for genetic matches who have Hugh Stone in their trees, but to identify and test known descendants of Hugh Stone.

Table 5, which is adapted from information provided by AncestryDNA,[14] shows the likelihood that testing a close relative will identify a DNA match who the original test-taker does not match. Second cousins and closer are not shown in this table, as the original test-taker will always match those relatives.

Table 5. Likelihood (in percentage) that testing a close relative will identify a DNA match with a third through seventh cousin who the original test-taker does not match (adapted from AncestryDNA)

Relationship	Sibling	Uncle/Aunt	Niece/Nephew	Parent	Grandparent	First Cousin	Second Cousin
3rd cousins	87	99	64	96	100	94	97
4th cousins	42	78	25	63	92	57	64
5th cousins	15	37	8	26	58	22	26
6th cousins	4	13	2	9	23	7	8
7th cousins	1.5	4	0.8	3	8	2	3

The information in this table can help identify which close relative to test in order to examine a specific genealogical question. For example, if the goal of a research project involving atDNA is to identify whether DNA is shared with a fourth cousin, the best close family member to test is a grandparent on that side of the family (with a 92 percent chance that the grandparent will match the fourth cousin), followed by an uncle or aunt (with a 78 percent chance of matching the fourth cousin). It is interesting to note that testing an aunt or uncle provides greater odds than testing a parent.

---

[14] "Should Other Family Members Get Tested?," AncestryDNA, *AncestryDNA Matching Help and Tips* (http://dna.ancestry.com); accessed from the AncestryDNA-match page, which is visible only to testers and test administrators.

Genetic Matches and Genetic Networks as Hints for New Research

In addition to supporting or rejecting a genealogical hypothesis, genetic genealogy test results can be used to identify clues for new lines of research. This is usually the result of mining genetic matches at the testing companies or in third-party databases, and is less frequently the result of target-testing close relatives.

Clues for genealogical research can come from genetic matches' profiles or shared information. A fourth cousin match at one of the testing companies might reveal a possible shared ancestor, for example, who can be researched. For very distant genetic matching it is often unclear whether shared DNA is a result of an identified common ancestor or an unknown common ancestor who may be shared between the trees, but finding a genealogical relative who may or may not be a genetic relative can be a boon for our research. Often these genealogical relatives have records or information that are not publicly available, such as stories, photographs, or Bibles with family members' birth, death, and marriage dates. Sometimes DNA can be a tool to build bridges with genealogical relatives.

In addition, match lists can be reviewed for significant clusters of surnames or groups. A group of relatively close genetic matches who may or may not be related to each other but seem to share ancestry in the same small town in rural Nebraska may suggest an ancestor or relative from that area. This could be of particular interest when previous research has led to that same small town. Although never conclusive evidence on its own, this clustering is highly exploitable and is likely to be the source of new tools or analyses in the future.

Testing companies also offer hints for new lines of research. DNA Circles and New Ancestor Discoveries at AncestryDNA, for example, use a combination of DNA-matching and publicly available family trees to try to create groups of descendants of a common ancestor or ancestral couple. Although these groupings are often the result of sharing DNA through lines other than that of the identified ancestor, they can provide clues for consideration and review. DNA Circles and New Ancestor Discoveries are based only on DNA sharing and Ancestry trees; they cannot be considered sufficient evidence of a relationship, but may be combined with other evidence to reach a sound conclusion.

Chromosome Mapping and Triangulation

A primary goal of atDNA testing is to identify the ancestor who provided a segment of DNA shared with a genetic match. Armed with such information, genetic matches can then trace that segment of DNA through both time and space.

Chromosome mapping is the process by which specific segments of DNA are assigned to specific ancestors. To map the segments, it is necessary to test or identify relatives who share both a segment of DNA and a known ancestor. For example, a test-taker who has also tested all four of her grandparents could easily map every single segment of her DNA to at least her grandparents' generation. For most test-takers, especially those without living or tested grandparents, segments are assigned to grandparents or more distant ancestors on a much smaller scale.

Triangulation is a process in which a group of three or more people who share a segment of DNA assign that segment to an ancestor found in each of their family trees. Chromosome mapping can be tentatively performed without triangulation when the relationship is sufficiently close—such as with first cousins who share a set of grand-parents—but for confirmation of tentative mapping and for more distant relationships, triangulation is usually considered very good supporting evidence. While random recombination may result in little or no shared or overlapping DNA segments between some cousins, when it is found, triangulation may offer more credible evidence of relationships. The extent to which triangulated segments support a hypothesis is still a matter of debate, with many genetic genealogists considering triangulation the gold standard.

Other genetic genealogists, in contrast, are concerned that segment triangulation is too fraught with potential difficulties to be considered strong evidence. For example, many genetic genealogists have embraced tree triangulation as an alternative to segment triangulation, particularly at AncestryDNA where segment data is currently not available to test-takers. Tree triangulation is the name given to the process of identifying com-monalities such as shared surnames or ancestors in the family trees of two or more close matches. However, this form of triangulation is subject to errors if the trees are not ac-curate and complete. Additional case studies incorporating DNA and accurate trees are necessary to provide clarity about the usefulness of DNA-segment triangulation.

The benefit of triangulation and chromosome mapping is identifying a part of the fam-ily tree to search for a shared ancestor. For example, when a test-taker has reliably mapped a DNA segment to a great-grandmother, the test-taker's matches who share that segment know they are related through that great-grandmother; the search for the com-mon ancestor can be limited to just one eighth of the test-taker's family tree.

After receiving atDNA test results, the process of mapping chromosome segments to specific ancestors can begin. The following steps outline the procedure.

Step 1: Downloading segment data

The first step in chromosome mapping and triangulation is to obtain information about the DNA segments shared with genetic matches, including the chromosome number and the location on that chromosome of the shared DNA. Segment data may be obtained as follows:

- **Family Tree DNA**—The test-taker can download segment data for each and every genetic match identified in the company's database using the "Down-load All Matches to Excel (CSV Format)" option in the Chromosome Browser tool.

- **23andMe**—This testing company provides the option to download segment data for matches, but only for those matches who have agreed to share genomes with the test-taker.

- **GEDmatch**—The One-to-One tool provides segment data for a single match; this data can be retained in a spreadsheet. Data for multiple kits may be obtained by finding genetic matches using the One-to-Many tool, then selecting kits of interest and using the option (on a subsequent analysis screen) to download a spreadsheet of all the segment data. Much of the data from *GEDmatch* can also be downloaded from Family Tree DNA and 23andMe.

- **DNAgedcom**—*DNAgedcom* provides an easier way to download data from Family Tree DNA and 23andMe. A client tool can also download total shared DNA data (but not segment data) from AncestryDNA.

Unfortunately, AncestryDNA does not provide segment data for matches. It is beneficial to ask genetic matches at AncestryDNA to create a profile at *GEDmatch* and upload their raw data there for comparison.

Step 2: Creating and adjusting a spreadsheet

After downloading the segment data, it can be organized and analyzed. Many genetic genealogists import the segment data into a single spreadsheet with columns for information such as match name, testing company, chromosome, start location, end location, centimorgans, relationship, e-mail address, and surnames. Many genetic genealogists use tools other than spreadsheets, such as DNAMatch for iPad and Genome Mate Pro, but the concepts involved with the analysis are the same. Specific tools are not covered here.

Segments included in the spreadsheet may be as small as 1 cM, but small segments are more likely to be false-positive matches.[15] Most genetic genealogists recommend using segments of at least 10 cM when analyzing atDNA, while some recommend 5 cM or 7 cM minimum. When working on endogamous populations segments smaller than 20 cM may be difficult to assign to a specific ancestor or ancestral couple. No matter the minimum size selected, larger segments are generally easier to analyze and assign. A general guideline would be to amend the spreadsheet by removing all segments below an established minimum, leaving the longest segments for triangulation.

Step 3: Sorting into potential triangulation groups

To create potential triangulation groups (groups of individuals who potentially all share a segment of DNA), the spreadsheet data should be sorted first by chromosome and then by start location. In table 6, for example, the test-taker shares a segment of DNA on chromosome 11 with four other people.

---

[15] Eric Y. Durand, Nicholas Eriksson, and Cory Y. McLean, "Reducing Pervasive False Positive Identical-by-De scent Segments Detected by Large-Scale Pedigree Analysis," *Molecular Biology and Evolution Advance Access*, 30 April 2014 (http://mbe.oxfordjournals.org/content/early/2014/04/30/molbev.msu151. full.pdf): 2; DOI: 10.1093/molbev/msu151.

Table 6. Overlapping segments of DNA

Match	Chromosome	Start Location	End Location	Centimorgans	SNPs
George Smith	11	40950451	70140411	19.50	5096
Craig Yancey	11	40950451	64369917	13.19	3896
June Wright	11	40950451	64369917	13.19	3896
Wilma Rye	11	48972954	70140411	17.58	4500

Sharing an overlapping segment of DNA with two or more people, as in table 6, does not automatically signify a triangulation group, as it is still unknown which members of the group share the DNA segment with one another. These initial groupings are only *potential* triangulation groups. Some of the members of a potential triangulation group may share the segment with the test-taker on the maternal chromosome, while other members of the potential triangulation group may share the segment with the test-taker on the paternal chromosome. These two groups would form two different—and almost certainly unrelated—triangulation groups.

Step 4: Identifying triangulation groups

The next step is to determine which members of a potential triangulation group share the overlapping segment of DNA with each other. There are several approaches to identifying true or likely triangulation groups.

- **Family Tree DNA**—The ICW and Matrix tools enable a test-taker to determine whether two genetic matches share *some* segment of DNA. For example, if the ICW or Matrix tool at Family Tree DNA reveals that George Smith and Wilma Rye in table 6 share *some* segment of DNA, it is likely but not certain that they share the segment identified on chromosome 11. George and Wilma could, for example, share a different segment of DNA. The ICW or Matrix tool at Family Tree DNA only allows for tentative triangulation-group formation.

  The ICW information in table 7, for example, suggests that there are actually two triangulation groups at this location of chromosome 11. The shaded boxes indicate the same person is named in both the row and column; the X indicates the person in the row and the person in the column share DNA. The first tentative triangulation group contains George Smith, Wilma Rye, and the unnamed test-taker. The second tentative triangulation group contains Craig Yancey, June Wright, and the unnamed test-taker.

- **23andMe**—The DNA Relatives tool (accessed by clicking on "Tools," then "DNA Relatives," then "DNA") enables a test-taker to compare the DNA of any two matches who have agreed to share genomes with the test-taker. Using this tool, a test-taker can identify which, if any, DNA segments two genetic matches share with one another.

Table 7. Matrix of genetic matches showing ICW status

	George Smith	Craig Yancey	June Wright	Wilma Rye
George Smith				X
Craig Yancey			X	
June Wright		X		
Wilma Rye	X			

- **GEDmatch**—Several tools at *GEDmatch* enable a user to compare DNA of two or more genetic matches. The One-to-One tool directly compares two sets of results and identifies shared DNA segments. The Triangulation tool, available to *GEDmatch* members who have made donations (known as Tier 1 members), identifies triangulation groups.

- **Contacting Matches**—Asking matches whether they share DNA with another—and, if so, what segments they share—can help identify triangulation groups.

As tentative and confirmed triangulation groups are identified, they can be sorted or noted on the spreadsheet.

Step 5: Working with triangulation groups

After a tentative or confirmed triangulation group is identified, the members of that group can work together to try to identify their shared ancestor or ancestors. That can be as simple as sharing and reviewing group members' family trees. When an ancestor is found in the trees of all group members, that ancestor can be tentatively identified as the source of the shared DNA segment.

Limitations of chromosome mapping and triangulation

Chromosome mapping and triangulation are not error-proof. They are highly susceptible to the possibility that a DNA segment could have been inherited from another ancestor, possibly one not known to be shared by the matching cousins. Anyone performing triangulation must consider this possibility.

Findings reported by AncestryDNA suggest that while there is about an 85 percent probability that three first cousins share at least one DNA segment, there is only a 15 percent chance that the same is true of three third cousins—and an almost zero percent chance that three or more fourth cousins will share at least one DNA segment.[16] Although this research has not yet been peer reviewed or published, it raises concerns about triangulation.

---

[16] "Do All Members of a DNA Circle Have the Same Matching Segment?," AncestryDNA, *Getting Started with DNA Circles* (http://dna.ancestry.com); accessed from the AncestryDNA-match page, which is visible only to test-takers and test administrators.

Members of a triangulation group should consider how much of their family trees is actually being compared when looking for a common ancestor. Trees with significant gaps in recent generations can be problematic, as matches could share ancestors that fall within those gaps.

A study by Ancestry.com of the completeness of family trees linked to AncestryDNA test results found that the trees were about 75 percent complete at the great-grandparent level, and just about 55 percent complete at the great-great-grandparent level.[17] By the fifth great-grandparent level, the trees were only about 10 percent complete. These trees are not the only ones that AncestryDNA members can or do compare, but the study demonstrates that the vast majority of trees are far from complete when looking back just a handful of generations. The study did not address tree accuracy, which is another critical requirement for sound genealogical analysis.

At a minimum it is important that genetic genealogists recognize and address the possibility that DNA could be shared through other lines.

Ethnicity Predictions

Ethnicity estimation—also known as admixture or biogeographical estimation—is the assignment of DNA segments to geographic areas based on comparisons of SNP results to one or more reference populations. SNPs are assigned to the reference population they most closely match. Ethnicity estimation, therefore, works based on the following principle:

> If sufficiently isolated for enough time, a population within a geographic region will become genetically distinct enough from neighboring populations such that individuals who share DNA similar to the genetically distinct DNA are likely to have come from that region.

Populations that were not sufficiently isolated will be too genetically similar to neighboring populations to be identifiable. The best populations for ethnicity estimation, therefore, are those that have been perfectly isolated for centuries or millennia—and who are willing to undergo DNA testing to create a reference population. Unfortunately, there are very few, if any, populations that have been perfectly isolated for centuries or millennia. Throughout history, DNA has been exchanged between neighboring towns, counties, and countries by migrants, travelers, invaders, and others. There is no perfectly isolated population and no perfect reference population.

Each of the testing companies has attempted to build scientifically-robust reference populations. These reference populations typically include hundreds or thousands of test-takers and combine research datasets with company-tested individuals. 23andMe has thirty-one reference populations built from public reference datasets (the 1000 Genomes project, HapMap, and the Human Genome Diversity Project) as well as from 23andMe test-takers with known ancestry. AncestryDNA's database includes individuals from

---

[17] Catherine A. Ball et al., "DNA Circles White Paper: Identifying Groups of Descendants Using Pedigrees and Genetically Inferred Relationships in a Large Database," *AncestryDNA* (http://dna.ancestry.com/resource/whitePaper/AncestryDNA-DNA-Circles-White-Paper.pdf).

twenty-six regions around the world. Family Tree DNA's reference database includes twenty-two clusters from regions across the globe. None of the testing companies have the same reference population database.

With a reference-population database in place, the testing companies can compare test-takers' DNA to those reference populations. This usually involves several steps. First, the company obtains a test-taker's raw data by testing or upload. The raw data is optionally processed by the company, including phasing and breaking the DNA sequence into segments. Each company uses an algorithm that compares a test-taker's raw data to the reference populations and assigns portions of the raw data to whichever reference population it most closely matches. Usually the algorithm involves a probability associated with each assignment; those probabilities can be used to make an overall ethnicity prediction. For example, a company may require a 50, 75, or 95 percent probability for a DNA segment before relying on that estimate. The segments are then reported individually (in the form of chromosomes) or as aggregate percentages. For example, 23andMe and *GEDmatch* attach ethnic labels to specific segments on chromosomes as well as providing percentages, while AncestryDNA and Family Tree DNA provide only percentages.

Third-party calculators

Testing companies are not the only places to obtain ethnicity estimates. *GEDmatch* offers a wide and growing variety of ethnicity calculators that analyze a test-taker's raw data. Each calculator has a slightly different focus, and, like other calculators, each uses a different reference population and has a slightly different algorithm.

One advantage of using *GEDmatch*'s ethnicity calculators is flexibility. Users have the ability to view results either in a chromosome browser display showing the segment assignments or as a percentage of aggregated ethnicities.

Limitations of ethnicity estimates

Two of the biggest complaints about ethnicity estimates are that (1) they vary from company to company, and (2) they do not match the expected estimate based on the genealogical family tree. Understanding ethnicity estimates and how they are obtained easily explains these two phenomena. Table 8 lists ethnicity estimates reported by the three testing companies for a single test-taker.

The estimates are relatively close but are not identical. They tend to deviate more as the regions become more specific, such as sub-regions or countries. There are several reasons why these estimates vary from company to company, including but not limited to the following:

1. **Different reference populations**. Each company has its own database of reference populations, which can have a significant impact on ethnicity assignments. Reference population databases have been refined several times by the testing companies, and this is expected to continue.

2. **Phased versus unphased raw data**. Phasing the raw data—assigning the DNA into one of two different chromosomes (one from each parent)—can

have an impact on ethnicity assignments, although not as significant an impact as different reference populations. Some companies do not phase the raw data before performing the ethnicity analysis.

Table 8. Ethnicity estimates in percentages for Blaine T. Bettinger, January 2016, as reported by the three major testing companies

Region	Percentage of DNA from this region		
	23andMe	AncestryDNA	Family Tree DNA
Africa	0.9	2	0
America	3.1	3	2
Asia	0	2	4
Europe	95.5	93	90

3. **Confidence levels**. The ethnicity estimate for every DNA segment is associated with a probability of the confidence in that assignment. Depending on the confidence-level threshold selected by the company, some ethnicities may not be reported to the test-taker. For example, an ethnicity estimate with a confidence level of 85 percent will not be reported if the company has decided to shows only ethnicity estimates above a 95 percent confidence level.

It is important to average or otherwise compare results across two or more calculators. Trying several different calculators to find the one that seems the most correct is not a scientific or supportable method; instead, two or more different calculators should be used to look for trends or common percentages. An accurate assignment should be reproducible in multiple calculators.

As discussed earlier, everyone has a genealogical family tree and a genetic family tree. Ethnicity estimates are obtained from DNA, considering only the ethnicity of the genetic family tree. A test-taker's genealogical family tree may have many ancestors from a particular region of the world, but if those ancestors are not part of the test-taker's genetic family tree, that region or ethnicity cannot be detected.

For these reasons, ethnicity estimates are subject to change over time as reference populations, algorithms, and other aspects of the analysis are refined.

Using ethnicity estimates
In addition to learning about the general populations in a test-taker's genetic family tree, when used with sufficient caution ethnicity estimates can also have more direct genealogical applications.

Adoptees, for example, can gain valuable information about genetic heritage using ethnicity estimates. An estimate of 30 percent Italian, for example, may suggest an Italian parent or grandparent. Similarly, an estimate of 50 percent Jewish would suggest a

Jewish parent. For an adoptee, this information can prove incredibly helpful in tasks such as narrowing down a list of potential candidates as parents or grandparents.

Ethnicity estimates may also be used for tentative chromosome mapping. If it is known where an ethnicity originated in a family tree, the segments linked to that ethnicity could be tentatively assigned to that source. For example, an individual with European ancestry who suspects a single ancestor with African and Native American ancestry within the past few generations could assign any African and Native American segments to that ancestor. Of course, the test-taker must always recognize and consider the possibility that the segments may have come from a different person.

Ethnicity estimates may assist in identifying an ancestor shared with a genetic match. Information provided by 23andMe includes start and stop locations for ethnicity assignments (found by viewing the "scientific details" on the page displaying ethnicity). Armed with this data, a test-taker who has identified a potential source of one of these segments based on assigned ethnicity can narrow the search for the common ancestor with someone that matches on that segment. For example, test-taker-1 and test-taker-2 share a DNA segment on chromosome 2, and both have a region of Native American ethnicity within that segment. If the test-takers believe that they share the chromosome with Native American DNA (rather than the other chromosome), they can look for overlap in their trees only where they believe the Native American ancestry originated. This, of course, is only a tentative process and is subject to several important limitations, the most important being the determination of whether the two test-takers share on the chromosome with the assigned ethnicity.

In conclusion, ethnicity estimates must be used with extreme caution. Although these estimates have improved considerably over the past few years, they may never reach the level where they can be accepted as definitive.

Chapter 5 Exercises

1. Sisters Karen (Johnson) Whitmore and Carrie (Johnson) Philips have received their results from an AncestryDNA test. The results indicate they are full sisters, sharing approximately 2,430 cM. When reviewing their genetic matches, Carrie notices that Karen shares a close match with an Ancestry user named "ThomasJohnson," who is predicted to be their third cousin with a possible range of third to fourth cousin. The user's tree reveals that "ThomasJohnson" is indeed their third cousin once removed. But when Carrie reviews her own results, she doesn't see "ThomasJohnson" as a match. Should Carrie expect "ThomasJohnson" to be in her match list? What could explain the absence?

2. Fred is testing numerous relatives in an attempt to map his chromosomes and characterize his genetic family tree. He does not share any detectable DNA with Victoria, a seventh cousin through shared fifth great-grandparents John and Helen Quincy. Can Fred conclude that John and Helen Quincy are not in his genetic family tree?

3. Roy and Mike share a single 6.43 cM DNA segment on chromosome 3. Of 23andMe, AncestryDNA, and Family Tree DNA, which company or companies will identify Roy and Mike as genetic relatives? Which company or companies will not identify Roy and Mike as genetic relatives?

4. One cM is equivalent to a 1 percent (one in one hundred) probability of a recombination event occurring somewhere within that DNA segment within a single generation. Is it possible to share a DNA segment of 100 cM or greater with a relative (other than a parent passing down entire chromosomes to a child)?

5. Viktor has tested his parents but not himself. His grandparents are living but he has not yet tested them because, he reasons, all the DNA he inherited from them was tested when Viktor tested his parents. He has an aunt, a first cousin, two second cousins, and a third cousin, all of whom are willing to test. Whom should Viktor test first?

_____

_____

_____

6. Sally has tested three of her grandparents. Her paternal grandfather is deceased and thus cannot be tested. The results show she shares the following amounts of DNA with her three tested grandparents:

	Paternal Grandmother	Maternal Grandfather	Maternal Grandmother
Amount of DNA Shared (%)	28.6	23.5	26.5

Based on this information, what percentage of DNA did Sally inherit from her untested paternal grandfather?

_____

_____

_____

The following is a chromosome-browser comparison of a paternal grandmother and her granddaughter, showing where they share DNA on chromosome 1. During meiosis, the father took the copies of chromosome 1 that he received from his father and from his mother and recombined—or didn't recombine—the chromosomes. The black box indicates the chromosome, and the shaded areas indicate the segments shared by the paternal grandmother and her granddaughter. Use the diagram to answer questions 7 and 8.

7. Place an arrow (or arrows) showing where the recombination must have occurred. How many recombination events occurred on chromosome 1?

_____

_____

_____

8. Draw on the following blank chromosome the segment or segments the grand-daughter would share with her paternal grandfather.

9. Laura has tested herself and her grandmother Brenda. On chromosome 4, they share the following DNA segments:

Laura has also tested her son Michael and would like to compare Michael's DNA to that of his great-grandmother Brenda. Which of the following chromosome-browser views might Laura expect to see when comparing Michael and Brenda?

a)

b)

c)

d)

Use the family tree chart titled "Relatives of Violet Redden" to answer questions 10 through 15.

Relatives of Violet Redden

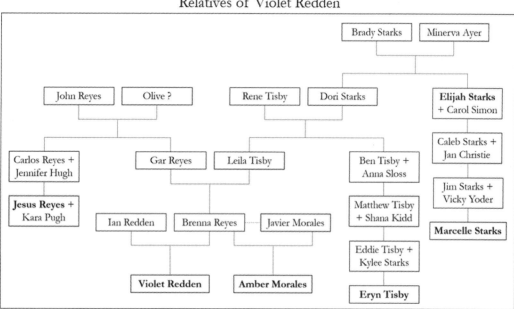

10. Violet Redden, the family genealogist, has tested herself as well as five family members (highlighted in **black** in the family tree). Complete the table below determining (a) relationship to Violet, and (b) expected amount of shared DNA (in percentage and in centimorgans). To determine relationship, use a search engine to locate "cousins charts" or use *Family Tree Magazine*'s "Relationship Chart" available online at http://www.familytreemagazine.com/upload/images/pdf/relationship.pdf. To determine the expected percentages, see Debbie Parker Wayne's "Percentage of Shared Autosomal DNA" quick-reference notes at http://debbiewayne.com/presentations/dna/ QuickRef_DNA_inherited_atDNA.pdf.

Relative	Expected Relationship to Violet Redden	Expected % of DNA in Common	Expected cM of DNA in Common
Jesus Reyes			
Amber Morales			
Eryn Tisby			
Elijah Starks			
Marcelle Starks			

11. Violet receives Eryn Tisby's results and discovers that Eryn shares 205 cM of DNA with Marcelle Starks. How does that result align with the family tree? If the result is unexpected, what piece of information from the tree might explain the result?

_____

_____

_____

Violet downloads her raw data and the raw data of Eryn Tisby, Elijah Starks, and Marcelle Starks. She uploads that raw data to *GEDmatch* to obtain information about the segments of DNA she shares with each of these relatives. The following table is a sample of some of the segments that Violet shares with Eryn, Elijah, and Marcelle. Use this table to answer questions 12 through 14.

Relative	Chromosome	Start Location	End Location	cM
Eryn Tisby	1	61687081	109171900	37.05
	5	14343689	26724511	12.58
	12	78977472	93650661	13.96
Elijah Starks	2	39940529	61792229	21.54
	18	11751127	36127946	18.9
	20	39812713	64231310	22.82
Marcelle Starks	8	11176816	16565963	10.56
	18	11751127	36127946	18.9

12. Determine the most distant ancestor or ancestors in the tree to whom the DNA segment that Violet shares with Elijah Starks on chromosome 18 can be tentatively mapped.

_____

_____

_____

13. Determine the ancestor or ancestors in the tree to whom the DNA segments that Violet shares with Eryn Tisby on chromosomes 1, 5, and 12 can be tentatively mapped

_____

_____

_____

14. Based on the information in the tree and the table, describe what is unusual about the DNA that Marcelle Starks shares with Violet.

_____

_____

_____

15. A chromosome browser reveals the following pattern on chromosome 5, with three genetic matches sharing a long segment of DNA (35 cM, 50 cM, and 75 cM) with the test-taker:

Based on this view, what do we know about the genetic relationship of each of the three individuals to one another?

_____

_____

_____

The following table was generated using segment data and Family Tree DNA's Matrix tool. The Matrix tool reveals whether two people share one or more DNA segments, but the tool does not reveal exactly what segment or segments are shared. In the table, shared DNA is indicated by an "x." Use this table to answer questions 16 and 17.

Chr	Start	End	cM	Name	Brenda	Ellen	Leonard	Susan	Johnny	Aaron	Georgia	Shana	Donna
1	207845978	247093448	57.02	Brenda			X					X	
1	231686686	236689066	11.11	Ellen				X	X		X		X
1	231875734	238703639	14.13	Leonard	X							X	
1	232679618	236689066	8.73	Susan		X			X		X		X
1	232679618	236689066	8.73	Johnny		X		X			X		X
1	233845007	236689066	6.32	Aaron									
1	234808789	234108935	18.43	Georgia		X		X	X				X
1	235328384	234108935	17.09	Shana	X		X						
1	235328384	243660729	18.66	Donna		X		X	X				

16. Place the nine individuals listed in the table into potential triangulation groups based on the segment data and the Matrix tool results.

_____

_____

_____

17. What is the limitation of using this approach for triangulation? What additional piece of information would you seek to verify that these potential groups are true triangulation groups?

_____

_____

_____

18. Using the table below, calculate the completeness of your genealogical family tree back at least seven generations (to sixth cousin relationships), where completeness is the percentage of ancestors for whom you have a name or some identifying information. Consider the reliability and accuracy of that information, especially in the generations where most distant-cousin relationships are being compared. How might this impact the search for shared ancestry with identified genetic matches? (The "Total # of Possible Ancestors" column may change if there have been recent cousin marriages.)

Generation	Matches	By Generation			
		Total # of Possible Ancestors	Total # of *Known* Ancestors	Total % of *Known* Ancestors	Total % of *Unknown* Ancestors
Grandparent	1st cousins	4			
G-Grandparent	2nd cousins	8			
2G-Grandparent	3rd cousins	16			
3G-Grandparent	4th cousins	32			
4G-Grandparent	5th cousins	64			
5G-Grandparent	6th cousins	128			

19. Angeline would like to identify the unknown parents of her fourth great-grandfather John Williams, who was born in Massachusetts in the 1750s, but she has nearly exhausted the documentary research and has found only a few clues. She has identified thirty-five living descendants of various sons of John Williams, although none are on the Y-DNA line; each of his sons' lines appears to have daughtered-out in the first few generations. Angeline wonders whether atDNA testing may reveal the identity of John Williams's parents. Can Angeline use atDNA for this research project? If not, why not? If so, how many descendants should she test?

_____

_____

_____

20. David Welch believes his great-great-grandfather George Smith was part Native American. There is no documentary evidence to support the belief, so David turned to atDNA testing in hopes of detecting Native American ethnicity. The testing company reported that he has no detectable amount of Native American ancestry. How does this result impact David's hypothesis?

_____

_____

_____

CHAPTER 6

Genealogical Applications for X-DNA

What is X-DNA?

The X chromosome is in the cell nucleus along with the autosomal chromosomes. An atDNA test usually includes SNPs on the X chromosome, therefore no separate test is necessary to obtain X-DNA results.

The X and Y chromosomes are known as the sex chromosomes. A man has one Y chromosome (inherited from his father) and one X chromosome (inherited from his mother). A woman has two X chromosomes (one from her father and one from her mother). The X chromosome inherited from the mother may be a recombination of the mother's two X chromosomes or it may be one of the mother's X chromosomes passed down intact. A father's X chromosome is always passed to his daughters intact, for he has no second X chromosome to recombine with the first.

X-DNA Inheritance Patterns

Figure 1 illustrates one possible route of X-DNA inheritance through three generations. The top row contains grandparents, the middle row contains parents, and the bottom row contains children. Random recombination and inheritance may result in the children inheriting a different combination of X-DNA than shown here. The X or XX beside each person represents the X-DNA inherited by that person from the previous generation. The numbers near the Xs help trace the path from the early generations to the later ones.

Grandparents (top row)

The paternal grandfather inherited one recombined X chromosome (X1) from his mother. The paternal grandmother inherited one unchanged X chromosome (X2) from her father and one recombined X chromosome (X3) from her mother.

The maternal grandfather inherited one recombined X chromosome (X4) from his mother. The maternal grandmother inherited one unchanged X chromosome (X5) from her father and one recombined X chromosome (X6) from her mother.

Parents (middle row)

The father did not inherit any X-DNA from his father. However he did receive a recombined mix of his mother's two X chromosomes (X2&3).

The mother inherited one unchanged X chromosome (X4) from her father. She also received a recombined mix of her mother's two X chromosomes (X5&6).

Children (bottom row)

The son did not inherit any X-DNA from his father. He did inherit an X chromosome (X5&6) from his mother. In this example, due to the randomness of recombination, the son did not inherit any of the mother's X4 chromosome, which she inherited from her father.

The daughter inherited one unchanged X chromosome (X2&3) from her father. She also inherited a recombined mix of her mother's two X chromosomes (X4&5&6).

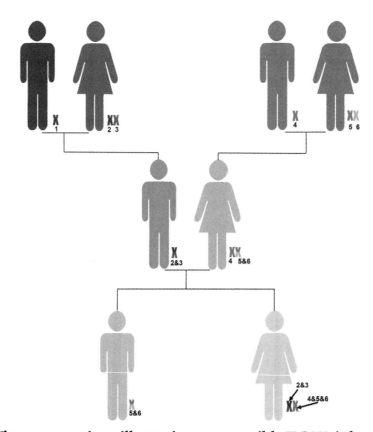

Figure 1. Three generations illustrating one possible X-DNA inheritance path

X-DNA Inheritance Charts

Because of the unique X-DNA inheritance pattern, concentration and practice are required to accurately trace X-DNA through a family. X-DNA inheritance charts simplify the analysis. These charts use color or shading to highlight the ancestors who may have contributed to a focus person's X-DNA. Those who are not shaded could not have contributed to the X-DNA of the focus person. Men and women have different X-DNA inheritance patterns, so it is imperative the correct chart be used based on the gender of the focus person. When analyzing a woman's X-DNA, use a chart designed for a female. When analyzing a man's X-DNA, use a chart designed for a male.

An Internet search will uncover multiple versions of X-DNA inheritance charts. Some genealogy software programs and DNA-analysis tools can create such charts. Several genetic genealogists have made versions available for others to use:

- Bettinger, Blaine. "More X-Chromosome Charts." *The Genetic Genealogist*. 12 January 2009. http://www.thegeneticgenealogist.com/2009/01/12/more-x-chromosome-charts/.
- Coakley, Louise. "X-DNA's Helpful Inheritance Patterns." *Genie1*. 12 June 2015. http://www.genie1.com.au/blog/63-x-dna#!kmt-start=0.
- [Griffith, Sue.] "Downloads." *Genealogy Junkie*. http://www.genealogyjunkie.net/downloads.html.
- [Turner, Jim.] "X Chromosome Inheritance." *Rootsweb*. http://freepages.genealogy.rootsweb.ancestry.com/~hulseberg/DNA/xinheritance.html.
- Wayne, Debbie Parker. "DNA Quick Reference Notes." *Deb's Delvings in Genealogy*. 13 February 2015. http://debsdelvings.blogspot.com/2015/02/dna-quick-reference-notes.html.

Most of the charts above include more than four generations.

Simplified versions of five-generation X-DNA inheritance charts are shown in figures 2 and 3. Ancestors who may have contributed to a test-taker's X-DNA are shaded. Those in unshaded boxes could not have contributed to the test-taker's X-DNA.

Although the shaded boxes in figures 2 and 3 demonstrate which ancestors *may* have contributed X-DNA to the test-taker, the ancestors who actually did contribute X-DNA to the test-taker will be a small subset of the shaded boxes. In many women the two X-chromosomes fail to recombine before the chromosome is passed on to a child. As a result, an entire line of shaded boxes—either a mother's line or a father's line—will be eliminated from the child's X-DNA genetic tree.

Advantages, Limitations, and Test Strategies for X-DNA

The unique inheritance pattern of X-DNA raises several important considerations, including the following:

- Sisters who share a father will always share an entire X chromosome, as he had only one X chromosome to pass on. Males do not inherit an X chromosome from their father, so this rule doesn't apply to men.
- Male and female siblings (other than identical twins) who have the same mother have three different options for sharing their **maternal** X chromosome: (1) they can share an entire maternal X chromosome, which will be either their maternal grandmother or maternal grandfather's X chromosome; (2) they can share one or more portions of their maternal X chromosome, which means there was recombination in one or both of them; or (3) they can

share absolutely no maternal X-DNA, due to receiving different X chromosomes from the mother. In a rare fourth option, siblings could share an entire X chromosome—or fail to share an entire X chromosome—if the mother's X chromosomes experienced recombination at the same location for each child.

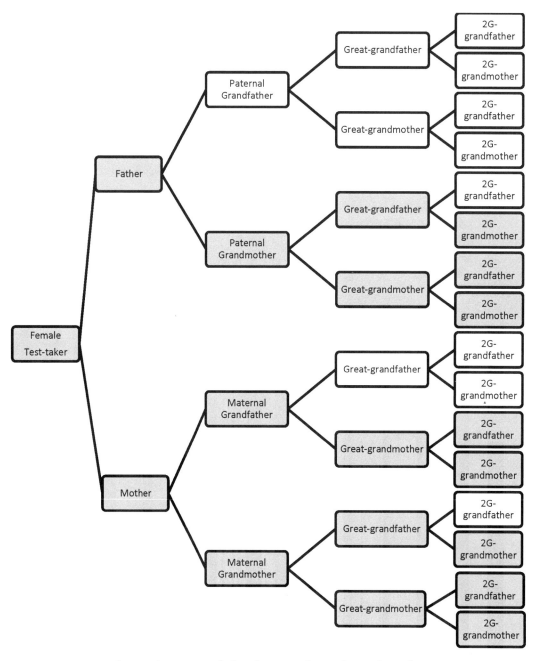

Figure 2. X-DNA inheritance chart for a female

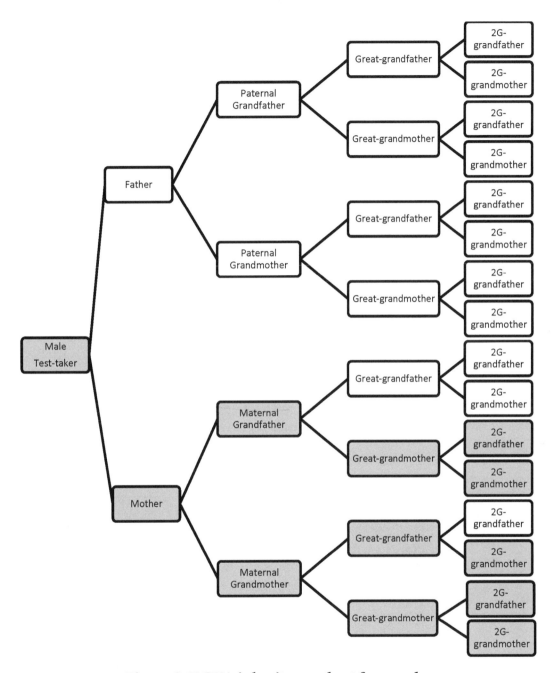

Figure 3. X-DNA inheritance chart for a male

X-chromosome matches are most often used in conjunction with atDNA matches to help narrow the focus to specific ancestral lines. Because some ancestors could not have contributed to a person's X-DNA, those lines can tentatively be ruled out from the search for a common ancestor. Genealogists should be aware that there are scenarios where a genetic match shares multiple ancestors, including one who provided matching atDNA and another who provided matching X-DNA.

X-DNA segments can be analyzed in the same way as atDNA—by looking for other test-takers who share overlapping segments and who share an ancestral line. Current studies indicate that X-DNA segments, just like atDNA segments, can persist for many generations. Careful analysis of the matching X-DNA segments is required before reaching any conclusion as to how many generations back a common ancestor may be. Some test-takers have many small matching segments on the X chromosome, which may come from common ancestors so far back in time that the link can never be established with documentary research.

When determining who to include in a match list, testing companies use thresholds for segment size and total amount of shared DNA. See the discussion in the chapter titled "Genealogical Applications for atDNA." Some testing companies incorporate shared X-DNA into the thresholds and some require matches to meet an atDNA-sharing threshold before considering X-DNA segments. Some companies use different X-DNA thresholds for males and females due to the different inheritances patterns. The *ISOGG Wiki* (http://isogg.org/wiki) is a good place to find current policies for any given company. Policies and thresholds may change as new DNA discoveries are made. If a testing company does not include shared X-DNA into matching algorithms, the only way to find a person who shares DNA *only* on the X chromosome is to use a third-party tool such as those available on *GEDmatch* (http://www.gedmatch.com).

In addition to the many benefits of testing and studying X-DNA, there are also several important limitations to its use. Just like every other type of DNA and any other record type, X-DNA inherently possesses characteristics that must be considered when utilizing the test results for genealogy:

- Due to the unique inheritance pattern of the X chromosome—namely the transmission of an entire unchanged X chromosome from every man to his daughters—the possible path of X-DNA must be considered more carefully than any other type of DNA.
- Men generally will have fewer matches on the X chromosome than women, in part because men have only one X chromosome, and in part because a man's X chromosome is naturally phased (segregated into paternal and maternal chromosomes), thus ruling out false positives.
- The absence of an X-DNA match does not rule out a relationship on a line through which X-DNA is inherited. Random recombination and inheritance can result in two people who are related on an X-DNA line sharing no X-DNA.

As in the case of atDNA, many genetic genealogists recommend using segments of at least 10 cM when analyzing X-DNA, while some recommend a minimum of 5 cM. Small segments can indicate a common ancestor on the X-inheritance lines, but the ancestor may be too far back in time to identify with documentary research. More multi-generation family-study results and better X-DNA testing are needed to determine the best value to use.

X-DNA Tools

The testing companies do not offer any tools specifically for X-DNA analysis, but most of the atDNA tools can be used on X-DNA data. Chromosome browsers can be used to examine shared X-DNA segments, including start and stop locations.

Specialized X-chromosome analysis tools are offered by third-party websites, where some atDNA tools also can be used on the X chromosome data:

- *DNAgedcom* (http://www.dnagedcom.com) has an Autosomal DNA Segment Analyzer that can be used on X chromosome data. The output is similar to that shown in figure 4.

CHROMOSOME X
36 matching segments
Longest is 85.40 cM, Graph = 297 KBP/pixel

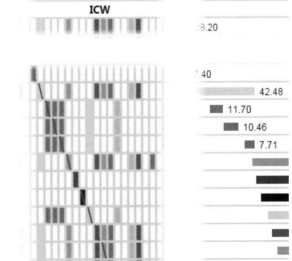

MAT	START	END	cM		ICW	
AC01	5697741	23009991	28.20			8.20
Ngiare	17130740	22594282	7.40			7.40
DP05	22803814	48226699	42.48			42.48
Myra I	30779417	36014147	11.70			11.70
Myra I	36225714	42108260	10.46			10.46
Myra I	44286773	48421735	7.71			7.71
DP04	47164938	94313371	24.56			
Angel	48724968	68235478	7.65			
Gail St	50504894	68420451	7.11			
Myra I	53161383	73727632	8.35			
e RAP01	54576388	92884070	16.69			
DP05	56846003	94313371	17.59			
: DJP01	68051531	94313371	14.85			

Figure 4. Sample output from DNAgedcom's Autosomal DNA Segment Analyzer

- *GEDmatch* (http://www.gedmatch.com) offers One-To-Many and One-To-One comparisons for X-DNA matches.

- Genetic Genealogy Kit (GGK) ("Tools," *Genetic Genealogy Tools*, http://www.y-str.org/p/tools-utilities.html), which can be downloaded and installed on a personal computer, analyzes a test-taker's raw data file. The atDNA tools in GGK also analyze the X chromosome.

- David Pike's Autosomal Analysis Tools (http://www.math.mun.ca/~dapike/ FF23utils/pair-comp.php) will read and operate on a data file, and will display the results, but will not store the data on a server. The atDNA tools also analyze the X chromosome or chromosomes when the data is in the uploaded file. The output is similar to the following:

> Chr X has a Single Segment Match of length 227 from position 21857819 to position 51001174 (29.14 Mb)
> Chr X has a Single Segment Match of length 843 from position 7779527 to position 85975955 (78.20 Mb) (2 non-matching SNPs treated as matching)
> Chr X has a Single Segment Match of length 498 from position 13781338 to position 132100527 (118.32 Mb) (1 non-matching SNPs treated as matching)

- Genome Mate Pro (http://genomemate.org), which may be installed and run on a personal computer, shows overlapping segments on the X and other chromosomes. The X-DNA functions are most useful when there are GEDCOMs for the DNA matches. With imported GEDCOM files for both test-takers, the tool can list potential common ancestors who may have contributed to the X-DNA of the genetic matches. The output for the overlapping DNA segments is similar to that shown in figure 5.

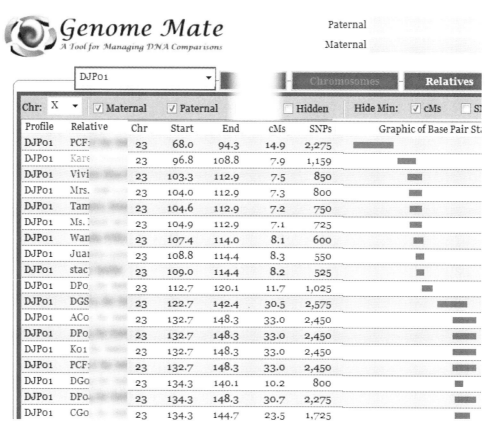

Figure 5. Sample output from Genome Mate

Applications for X-DNA segment analysis

A matching X-DNA segment of a significant size (say 10 cM or longer) allows the search for a common ancestor to focus on a line that may have contributed to the X-DNA of the two test-takers. This eliminates the need to search ancestral lines that could not have contributed X-DNA. For example, a male test-taker who shares a significantly-sized segment of X-DNA with another person can focus only on his maternal line when looking for the common ancestor. If that male test-taker's X-DNA match is to another male, half of each test-taker's family tree can be eliminated from consideration, resulting in less research.

The absence of a match on the X chromosome does not indicate that research should focus only on lines from which X-DNA could not have been inherited. The common ancestor could still be in the X-DNA inheritance path if random recombination eliminated detectable shared DNA segments.

Chapter 6 Exercises

Use the family tree chart in Appendix A titled "Descendants of John Ira Jones and Mary Ann (Smith) Jones" to answer questions 1 through 7. The genealogist has confirmed that there are no common ancestors for the people named on the chart other than those shown. Each kinship link has been confirmed with strong documentary evidence.

Hint: The easiest way to answer these questions is to make a copy of the chart, then, beginning with Mary Ann Smith, uniquely mark all descendants who may have inherited X-DNA from her. Next move to John Ira Jones and uniquely mark all descendants who might have inherited X-DNA from him. Continue moving to people who married into the family and repeat the process for each, using a different mark for each person.

Each question considers only the ancestors shown on the chart. In real situations, lines not shown on the chart must also be considered, but space does not allow inclusion of in-depth trees for every person named in this exercise. In a real scenario, the same analysis used to answer the questions about the ancestors on the chart would be applied to the complete family trees of all persons involved in the research problem.

In the following questions, a parenthesized number after an individual's name represents that person's number on the chart.

1. Which ancestors shown may have contributed to the X-DNA of Ira Gerball (20)?

2. Which ancestors shown may have contributed to the X-DNA of Mandella Louise Smith (33)? Would Mandella have inherited X-DNA from all of these possible ancestors?

3. Does Louis Gerball (32) share an X-DNA inheritance line with Mandella Louise Smith (33) through the ancestors shown on this chart?

4. Does Ira Ryan (43) share an X-DNA inheritance line with Mandella Louise Smith (33) through the ancestors shown on this chart?

_____

_____

_____

5. Does Viola Scott (17) share an X-DNA inheritance line with Ellis Jones (10) through the ancestors shown on this chart?

_____

_____

_____

6. Given the following X-DNA match results for Mandella Louise Smith (33), is the shared-segment size large enough for a genealogist to focus research for a common ancestor on those who could have contributed to the X-DNA of the test-takers? Start and stop locations have been rounded.

Name	Chr	Start	Stop	cM	SNPs
Emmy Wick (34)	X	92.7	122.4	32.00	3,450
Violet Sweets (29)	X	103.3	112.9	7.53	850
Janice Johns (31)	X	104.6	112.9	7.15	750

_____

_____

_____

7. Which ancestors shown on the chart are potential common ancestors who could have contributed the matching X-chromosome segment?

_____

_____

_____

8. An X-DNA segment of a significant size is shared by Debbie, Debbie's full brother, and test-taker Allen Jackson. On which portions of the trees of these test-takers should the search for a common ancestor focus?

_____

_____

_____

9. An X-DNA segment of a significant size is shared by Debbie, Debbie's half-brother (son of Debbie's mother), and test-taker Allen Jackson. On which portions of the trees of these test-takers should the search for a common ancestor focus?

_____

_____

_____

10. An X-DNA segment of a significant size is shared by Debbie, Debbie's half-brother (son of Debbie's father), and test-taker Allen Jackson. On which portions of the trees of these test-takers should the search for a common ancestor focus?

_____

_____

_____

CHAPTER 7

Incorporating DNA Testing in a Family Study

Incorporating Multiple Types of DNA Testing

Due to random mutations, recombination, and inheritance patterns, there are cases where one type of DNA test will not provide enough credible evidence to answer a genealogical question—even when combined with documentary evidence. In such situations it is often possible to test multiple types of DNA to more credibly support a conclusion.

Autosomal DNA test results are often combined with results from X-DNA or Y-DNA tests. A Y-DNA test may show, for example, that two men are recently related on their patrilineal line, with Family Tree DNA's TiP calculator showing 95 percent likelihood that they share an ancestor within the past seven generations—within a timeframe that atDNA testing might help. If the two men take an atDNA test and discover they are predicted third cousins, they have potentially identified the generation in which their common patrilineal ancestor lived. The sharing of atDNA by these two men does not prove they inherited that DNA from the common patrilineal line, but it is a reasonable hypothesis that could be pursued. In contrast, if a TiP calculation shows a 12 percent likelihood of a common ancestor within the past seven generations, atDNA-sharing may not help identify or narrow down the patrilineal relationship.

X-DNA—considered carefully—can also be a helpful test to combine with atDNA. As with all cases combining multiple types of DNA testing, genealogists must be careful not to simply conclude that a match who shares atDNA and X-DNA received all the matching DNA from the same ancestor. It is equally possible that the matching segments could have come from different ancestors, even from different sides of the family. That caveat aside, significant X-DNA-sharing can provide clues about where to look for a common ancestor. For example, a genetic match who shares a total of 150 cM of atDNA and a 45 cM segment of X-DNA is undoubtedly a very close relative, likely a second cousin or a second cousin once removed. Given the significant X-DNA matching, focus should initially be placed on the two individuals' X-DNA inheritance lines.

Due to its relatively slow mutation rate, mtDNA is not as commonly combined with other types of DNA testing, but its usefulness should not be overlooked. As mentioned in the mtDNA chapter, mtDNA provides critical evidence in some genealogical questions. When attempting to identify the parents of a female ancestor, mtDNA test results of suspected matrilineal descendants can provide evidence to confirm or disprove hypotheses. When combined with atDNA, X-DNA, or both types of testing, mtDNA test results can be even more useful. If a close matrilineal relationship is suspected and mtDNA evidence supports that hypothesis, atDNA testing can potentially shed additional light. The reverse is also true, especially as the size of atDNA databases continues to grow. If a close relationship is detected through atDNA-matching, and a matrilineal relationship is suspected based on documentary evidence, then mtDNA testing could provide helpful evidence.

Similarly, lack of atDNA-sharing between mtDNA matches suggests a relationship more distant than second cousins, while evidence of atDNA sharing suggests—but does not alone prove—a more recent common matrilineal ancestor. Possible sharing of atDNA through other lines must always be considered.

Table 1 shows examples of how two types of DNA tests can work together. The matrix is not exhaustive. In some cases a DNA test cannot be combined with other types of DNA, while in other cases three or four different types of DNA tests may be combined.

Table 1. Examples of situations employing two types of DNA tests

	mtDNA matching	Y-DNA matching	atDNA matching	X-DNA matching
mtDNA matching		Seldom used together regarding a single relationship; could be utilized to show that two males may be full brothers (sharing same Y-DNA and mtDNA)	atDNA-matching could provide evidence that mtDNA-sharing is due to a recent relationship; mtDNA-matching could suggest that atDNA cousins may be related on the matrilineal line	X-DNA-matching could provide evidence that mtDNA-sharing is due to a recent relationship; mtDNA-matching could suggest which of the possible X-DNA lines to investigate for a common ancestor
Y-DNA matching	Seldom used together regarding a single relationship; could be utilized to show that two males may be full brothers (sharing same Y-DNA and mtDNA)		atDNA-matching could provide evidence that Y-DNA-sharing is due to a recent relationship; Y-DNA-matching could suggest that atDNA cousins may be related on the patrilineal line	Seldom used together regarding a single relationship, as a male inherits Y from his father and X from his mother; could indicate matching on multiple lines
atDNA matching	mtDNA-matching could suggest that atDNA cousins may be related on the matrilineal line; atDNA-matching could provide evidence that mtDNA-sharing is due to a recent relationship	Y-DNA-matching could suggest that atDNA cousins may be related on the patrilineal line; atDNA-matching could provide evidence that Y-DNA-sharing is due to a recent relationship		X-DNA-matching could narrow a search for an ancestor shared with an atDNA match to specific lines on the tree
X-DNA matching	mtDNA-matching could suggest which of the possible X-DNA lines to investigate for a common ancestor; X-DNA- matching could provide evidence that mtDNA- sharing is due to a recent relationship	Seldom used together regarding a single relationship, as a male inherits Y from his father and X from his mother; could indicate matching on multiple lines	X-DNA-matching could narrow a search for an ancestor shared with an atDNA match to specific lines on the tree	

Combining multiple DNA types requires in-depth knowledge of every type of DNA test, including their limitations. As long as the possibility of sharing DNA through multiple lines is considered, using multiple types of DNA testing can provide helpful clues about where to look for common ancestry.

Each piece of documentary evidence can help confirm or refute a genealogical hypothesis. Each piece of DNA evidence can do the same. Correlating all the applicable evidence provides the most credible answer to any genealogical question. The exercises in this chapter illustrate how combining multiple types of DNA and complex analysis can provide added levels of credibility in the resulting conclusion.

Supporting or Refuting a Paper Trail with DNA

When used properly, DNA is just one piece of a genealogical puzzle. It is a record type just as census records, deeds, and military records are record types. Just as a single deed or census record alone cannot reconstruct a genealogical relationship, shared DNA should never be the sole piece of evidence used to support a conclusion. Instead, DNA is always combined with other evidence. Even in the instance of DNA confirming or revealing a parent/child relationship—where the least amount of non-DNA evidence would be required—there is always some documentary evidence. For example, the test-takers' names and the circumstances surrounding the birth are pieces of documentary evidence. DNA is added to documentary evidence not because it is considered to be more accurate (although in many cases it can be), but because it is another record type that can be used to test a hypothesis. DNA is being increasingly used to support or refute documentary evidence.

In science, a hypothesis with a significant amount of supporting evidence becomes a theory or law; in genealogy, a hypothesis with a significant amount of supporting evidence becomes a proof or conclusion. A genealogical conclusion is never final. Instead, a conclusion will continue to be tested with any new evidence that becomes available.

The amount of DNA needed to support a hypothesis can be very small, such as a single segment of atDNA, or it can be major, such as an atDNA project involving numerous descendants of an ancestor or ancestral couple.

Often the DNA evidence will conflict with documentary evidence. Misattributed-parentage events—where the biological parent or parents are different from those documented or expected—have occurred throughout history. Even well-documented family trees can be incorrect due to misattributed-parentage events. Every scientific study that examines misattributed parentage has found it occurring at the rate of usually around 1–2 percent of DNA transmissions in a given generation.[1] This means that for every one hundred

---

[1] See, for example, M. H. D. Larmuseau et al., "Low Historical Rates of Cuckoldry in a Western European Human Population Traced by Y-chromosome and Genealogical Data," *Proceedings of the Royal Society B: Biological Sciences* 280, no. 1772, December 2013; accessed online (http://rspb.royalsocietypublishing.org /content/280/1772/20132400); DOI: 10.1098/rspb.2013.2400.

children, approximately one or two are not offspring of the identified parents. These studies have utilized Y-DNA, as it can provide an easier answer for multi-generational studies, but the statistics should not be limited to father/son DNA-transmission events.

The amount of DNA required to refute a hypothesis can be very small or very large. Two atDNA tests that reveal an expected parent and child do not share DNA is usually sufficient to refute other evidence (for example, birth certificate, family interviews) that they are biologically parent and child. In contrast, the amount of DNA testing required to disprove a biological relationship from the 1600s or 1700s is significant, and there will often never be enough descendants to test. Lack of DNA-sharing among descendants is usually not evidence of a lack of a relationship, unless those descendants are second cousins or closer.

DNA evidence that appears to refute a hypothesis must be correlated with all other evidence. The following story illustrates this concept. In 2014, researchers at the University of Leicester reported on a study analyzing the mtDNA and Y-DNA of a skeleton believed to be that of King Richard III (1452–1485).[2] The study found that the skeleton's mtDNA matched that of a matrilineal descendant of Richard's sister, Anne of York. All the documentary evidence supported the conclusion that the skeleton was Richard's—location, battle wounds, and extreme scoliosis, for example. Researchers found that the Y-DNA extracted from the skeleton belonged to a completely different haplogroup than the Y-DNA of patrilineal descendants of Richard's great-great-grandfather King Edward III (1312–1377). This substantial finding seemed to contradict any conclusion that the skeleton was that of Richard III. However, twenty-four to twenty-six generations separated King Richard and the five male relatives tested, more than enough time for a misattributed-parentage event to break the line. Indeed, one of the five males tested did not match the other four, indicating a non-paternal event in that line within the past four generations. The study ultimately concluded that there was a greater than 99 percent probability that the skeleton was that of King Richard III, in spite of the Y-DNA evidence.

DNA evidence can be compelling, but it should never be accepted as definitive evidence without being reviewed in the greater context of the documentary evidence.

---

[2] Turi E. King et al., "Identification of the Remains of King Richard III," *Nature Communications* 5 (2014); accessed online (http://www.nature.com/ncomms/2014/141202/ncomms6631/full/ncomms6631.html); DOI: 10.1038/ncomms6631.

Chapter 7 Exercises

Use the family tree chart in Appendix A titled "Descendants of Henry Smith" to answer questions 1 through 7. The genealogist has confirmed that there are no common ancestors for the people named on the chart other than those shown. Each kinship link has been confirmed with strong documentary evidence, except where indicated in the exercises.

Shaded marker names in the Y-STR tables represent fast-moving markers. Markers not displayed in the table are assumed to match exactly on all men tested.

In the following questions, a parenthesized number after an individual's name represents that person's number on the chart.

1. Family legend indicates Henry Smith (1) married a Native American Choctaw woman. There are five generations between that woman and the descendants at the end of each line. While an atDNA test would likely indicate some Native American DNA in at least some of the descendants, there is a possibility the Native American atDNA was lost to random recombination and inheritance patterns. An mtDNA test could provide definitive proof if there is a living descendant who inherited the woman's mtDNA. Assuming only the end-of-line descendants (the last person or persons in each column) are still living, is there anyone living who inherited the mtDNA of the unknown spouse (2) of Henry Smith (1)?

_____

_____

_____

2. Assume a living person is found and agrees to test, and that the results indicate the mtDNA haplogroup is U5b1d1. Does this confirm or refute the family legend that Henry's unknown spouse (2) was Choctaw?

_____

_____

_____

3. Assuming only the end-of-line descendants are still living, is there anyone living who may have inherited the Y-DNA of Henry Smith (1)?

_____

_____

_____

4. George Smith (4) is believed to be the son of Henry Smith (1). The documentary evidence is weak and there are two George Smiths of the same general age in the same location at the same time. The goal is to prove that George Smith (4) is the son of Henry Smith (1). Two men—Ira Smith (43) and Robert Smith (33)—take a 37-marker Y-DNA STR test. Partial results are shown in the table below. Robert also took a SNP test. The two men have different haplogroups displayed. Does this mean there is no way they can be related? It may be helpful to reference the 2015 version of the ISOGG Y-DNA Haplogroup R Tree (http://isogg.org/tree/ISOGG_HapgrpR15.htm) to answer this question.

Test-taker	Haplo-group	DYS 393	DYS 390	...	DYS 449	DYS 464	...	DYS 607	...	CDY	...
Ira (43)	R-M512	13	25		31	12-15-15-16		14		35-39	
Robert (33)	R-M198	13	25		31	12-15-16-16		14		35-38	

Analysis of the STR-marker values may provide more evidence to answer the questions. Correlate the STR-marker values from the table above with the "Descendants of Henry Smith" tree.

5. Ira and Robert do not match on markers DYS464 and CDY. As explained in the Y-DNA chapter, two test-takers are related when they differ on two to three markers at 37 markers tested. Does this prove that George Smith (4) is the son of Henry Smith (1)?

6. Research continues by testing more descendants of Henry Smith (1), with the results shown in the table below. Describe the significance of the marker differences as related to the goal of determining whether Henry Smith (1) could be the father of George Smith (4). Note: It is not indicated in this table, but all other men in the Smith Surname Project who carry similar haplotypes to these men have marker DYS607=15. Use this data to answer this question's sub-parts.

Test-taker	Haplo-group	DYS 393	DYS 390	...	DYS 449	DYS 464	...	DYS 607	...	CDY	...
Ira (43)	R-M512	13	25	...	31	12-15-15-16	...	14		35-39	...
Robert (33)	R-M198	13	25	...	31	12-15-16-16	...	14		35-38	...
Louis Jr. (44)	R-M512	13	25	...	30	12-15-16-16	...	14		35-39	...
Bobby (45)	R-M512	13	25	...	31	12-15-16-16	...	14		35-39	...
Alfred Jr. (46)	R-M512	13	25	...	31	12-15-16-16	...	14		35-39	...

a. All tested descendants of Henry (1) share DYS607=14. What does this tell us about Henry (1)?

b. All tested descendants of Henry (1) share DYS607=14. What does this tell us about Ira (43)?

c. All descendants of Henry Jr. (5) have marker DYS464=12-15-16-16, while Ira (43) has DYS464=12-15-15-16. What does this tell us about a potential link between Henry (1) and George (4)?

d. Marker DYS449=30 for Louis Jr. (44), but DYS449=31 for the other tested men. What does this tell us about where this change may have occurred?

e. Marker CDY=35-38 for Robert (33), but CDY=35-39 for the other tested men. What does this tell us about where this change may have occurred?

_____

_____

_____

f. When all of the differences are counted, there are three markers that vary between these men (DYS464, DYS449, and CDY). As stated earlier, a fourth difference is seen in DYS607 between these men and others who are in the same group in the Smith Surname Project. When four differences exist at 37 tested markers, test-takers are "distantly related," while three differences would indicate test-takers are "related." Are there other factors to incorporate in the analysis?

_____

_____

_____

g. Could additional DNA testing provide more evidence to apply to this research question?

_____

_____

_____

7. All of the living cousins (those listed last in each line on the chart) agree to take an atDNA test. The table below shows selected fields of the cousins' entries from the match list of Ira Smith (43).

Selected atDNA match list items for Ira Smith (43), accessed 21 July 2014			
Match	Total Shared DNA (cM)	Longest Segment (cM)	Predicted Relationship
Robert Smith (33)	115.51	25.49	2nd to 4th cousin
Tommy Curtis (41)	80.01	33.63	2nd to 4th cousin
Edward Walker (42)	38.50	11.58	4th to remote cousin
Louis Smith Jr. (44)	60.76	13.34	3rd to 5th cousin
Bobby Smith (45)	35.13	8.15	5th to remote cousin
Alfred Smith Jr. (46)	41.92	9.06	5th to remote cousin

a. Is this a reasonably sized group of test-takers to possibly lead to credible conclusions about relationships?

_____

_____

_____

b. What might be a first step in analysis?

_____

_____

_____

c. Should we be concerned about the depth and accuracy of the test-takers' trees?

_____

_____

_____

d. Using the information in the table above, what might be a next step in our analysis?

_____

_____

_____

The table below is a matrix indicating which cousins show as "In Common With" each other.

In-Common-With matrix for the Smith cousins (manually created to include all test-takers)							
	Ira (43)	Robert (33)	Tommy (41)	Edward (42)	Louis Jr. (44)	Bobby (45)	Alfred Jr. (46)
Ira (43)	SELF	Yes	Yes	Yes	Yes	Yes	Yes
Robert (33)	Yes	SELF	Yes	Yes	Yes	Yes	Yes
Tommy (41)	Yes	Yes	SELF	Yes	Yes	Yes	Yes
Edward (42)	Yes	Yes	Yes	SELF	Yes	Yes	Yes
Louis Jr. (44)	Yes	Yes	Yes	Yes	SELF	Yes	Yes
Bobby (45)	Yes	Yes	Yes	Yes	Yes	SELF	Yes
Alfred Jr. (46)	Yes	Yes	Yes	Yes	Yes	Yes	SELF

> e. Using the information in the table, what might be a next step in our analysis?

_____

_____

_____

The table below shows selected elements of the resulting segment analysis. Small segments and matches from others not shown in this family chart have been eliminated. The items grouped at the top of the table would be found while logged in to the account of Ira Smith (43); his name is in the left column. The items grouped at the bottom of the table would be found while logged in to the account of Edward Walker (42); his name is in the left column.

Tested person	Match Name	Chr	Start	Stop	cM	SNPs	Rel
	**Shared-segment details for selected segments for Ira Smith (43) and cousins, and for Edward Walker (42) and cousins**						
Ira (43)	Tommy (41)	6	135113519	160850541	33.63	7101	4C
Ira (43)	Robert (33)	6	134769313	151510948	19.33	4154	3C1R
Ira (43)	Edward (42)	6	151306471	158850732	11.58	2290	4C
Ira (43)	Robert (33)	7	27322710	47468816	25.49	5563	3C1R
Ira (43)	Edward (42)	7	27723126	34259818	8.72	1984	4C
Ira (43)	Louis Jr. (44)	7	27322710	36912091	13.34	2881	4C
Ira (43)	Bobby (45)	7	25785734	30894793	8.15	1583	4C
Ira (43)	Alfred Jr. (46)	7	25785734	31479397	9.06	1784	4C
Edward (42)	Ira (43)	6	151306471	158850732	11.58	2290	4C
Edward (42)	Tommy (41)	6	151306471	158850732	11.58	2290	3C
Edward (42)	Robert (33)	6	Note 1				3C1R
Edward (42)	Ira (43)	7	27723126	34259818	8.72	1984	4C
Edward (42)	Robert (33)	7	27723126	34259818	8.72	1984	3C1R
Edward (42)	Louis Jr. (44)	7	27723126	34259818	8.72	1984	4C
Edward (42)	Bobby (45)	7	Note 1				4C
Edward (42)	Alfred Jr. (46)	7	Note 1				4C
	Note 1. No shared segment is shown, but the cousins' names are included here so the list is complete. The overlapping segment may have been among the small segments removed before beginning analysis. This can be confirmed by checking the detailed shared-segment data without removing the small segments.						

f. Using the information in the table above, what might be the next step in our analysis?

_____

_____

_____

Incorporating DNA Evidence in a Written Conclusion

One of the most important goals of genealogical research is the preservation and dissemination of conclusions about identities and relationships. Unless these conclusions are preserved—whether for a single relative or for thousands of readers of a genealogical journal—the research and effort will be lost, and future generations will be doomed to repeat the work. Most genealogical proofs require a discussion of evidence—something that cannot be completely and accurately conveyed in charts. Instead, genealogists must present the evidence and reasoning in a coherent, written form.

The current generation of genealogists faces a new challenge, namely incorporating the discussion of DNA evidence into genealogical writings. Genealogists must understand how to correlate DNA evidence with documentary evidence to analyze a genealogical question, and they must also understand how to present DNA evidence as one of the elements supporting a conclusion. Genealogists who are not yet using DNA in their own writings must grasp enough of the subject to be able to evaluate the writings of peers who are incorporating DNA.

The Genetic Genealogy Standards

The Genetic Genealogy Standards provide guidance for using DNA evidence in publications and presentations. These standards were drafted to help genealogists incorporate DNA effectively and to minimize misunderstandings and conflict. They describe best practices that all researchers should follow when purchasing, recommending, sharing, or writing about the results of DNA testing for genealogical research.[1] In particular, the standards related to privacy, interpretation, and sharing of DNA test results are important when creating a written conclusion.

Privacy Concerns

Some of the major concerns about DNA and privacy surround DNA's connection to medical information.

DNA does have a major impact on a person's health, however few medical conditions do or do not develop as the result of one individual gene variant. Most medical conditions are the result of a complex interaction of multiple gene variants and environmental

---

[1] *Genetic Genealogy Standards* (http://www.geneticgenealogystandards.com/).

conditions. A person's diet and exercise routine as well as habits, such as smoking and drinking, can affect the development of a particular condition. Because of all these factors, it is often difficult to predict the likely impact of any particular gene variant. Some geneticists believe that except for those few conditions where one gene variant alone determines whether a person will develop the medical condition, it is safe to share all DNA data. Unfortunately, a large percentage of the public does not understand the relatively weak association between DNA and health. Often too much significance is given to, for example, a single SNP that indicates a slight increase in a person's likelihood to develop a particular condition.

Family members may not agree about what genetic information should be publicly revealed. When one family member publicly shares his or her DNA data, information that applies to family members may also be revealed. For example, a test-taker shares 50 percent of his DNA with each of his parents, siblings, and children. If the test-taker reveals medically significant findings, there is a 50 percent chance that the same medical condition applies to the parents, siblings, and children. Based on what is now known about DNA and SNPs tested for genealogical purposes, the risk of revealing medically significant information is low, but it does exist. There is also a chance that a scientific discovery could find a new association between a medical condition or trait and a DNA segment that is currently being tested.

Ethically, each DNA-test-taker should consider his or her own beliefs as well as the thoughts and feelings of family members when making decisions about who to test and what data to share.

Sharing DNA Test Results

Ideally, a test-taker whose DNA information is used as evidence in a genealogical study will have granted permission to share the data and the test-taker's name. When arranging for a test or tests to be conducted, it is helpful to obtain the test-taker's written permission to share information. Almost all proof discussions involving DNA evidence will require details about DNA segments, markers, or locations. Without the test-taker's permission to share, a pseudonym is sometimes necessary.

Proof discussions involving atDNA may reveal the total amount of DNA shared, longest block shared, locations of shared segments (identified by chromosome numbers and start- and stop-points), and admixture estimates. For Y-DNA testing, discussions may include haplogroup, number of markers tested, marker names, and marker values. If mtDNA was tested, a written conclusion may disclose haplogroup, test resolution (HVR or full mtDNA sequence), and differences from a reference sequence. In all cases involving DNA test results, a portion of the test-taker's family tree will be shared to illustrate relationships.

Citing DNA Test Results

Elements that should be included in a citation involving DNA test results—and example citations—can be found in *Quicksheet: Citing Genetic Sources for History Research, Evidence Style,* and in various "QuickLessons" posted online at *Evidence Explained: Historical Analysis, Citation & Source Usage.*[2]

Suggested citation elements for DNA evidence include the following:
- Name of the test-taker, kit number, user name, user ID[3]
- Contact information (e-mail, postal address) for the kit manager
- For testing companies that issue a printed report, report name and date, along with name and address of person holding the report on a given date
- For dynamic reports viewed online, database name, selection criteria, and access date
- Names and contact information for individuals on a test-taker's match list
- Name, address, and URL of the testing company; if applicable, the lab that conducted the testing (as sometimes companies switch labs)
- Type, resolution, and pertinent version numbers of DNA-test taken
    - o Y-DNA: test name, marker names, number of STRs or SNPs tested
    - o mtDNA: test name, resolution (HVR1, HVR2, full mtDNA sequence)
    - o atDNA and X-DNA: test name, version or test date (if applicable)
    - o Whole genome sequence or full genome sequence, coverage level, and number of markers tested
- Details of shared DNA markers, percentages, predictions, segments
- Database name, database provider name, URL
- Background data for the database (for example, reference populations for admixture comparisons, build number used in the database)

Citations in research notes usually include more detail than those published in an article. Researchers may need the above elements in their research-note citations to allow for a complete and thorough analysis of the genetic information—even if some elements are not used when the work is published. Ethics, privacy policies, and legal restrictions may require that some suggested items be omitted or privatized for publication or distribution online or in a presentation, journal article, client report, or report that may be distributed to others. Some of these elements may increase in importance as new testing companies and new tests become available or as databases or tools disappear or change.

The exact details to include in a citation vary, depending on what is stated in the narrative. If shared-DNA information is not incorporated into the discussion, it should be

---

[2] Elizabeth Shown Mills, *Quicksheet: Citing Genetic Sources for History Research, Evidence Style* (Baltimore, MD: Genealogical Publishing, 2015). ———, *Evidence Explained: Historical Analysis, Citation & Source Usage* (https://www.evidenceexplained.com/); in particular see "QuickLesson 21: Citing DNA Evidence: Five Ground Rules" (https://www.evidenceexplained.com/content/quicklesson-21-citing-dna-evidence-five-ground-rules) and other lessons that may be applicable to DNA.

[3] Passwords may be needed for access, but they should not be shared publicly. Names of living test-takers should not be shared without permission, unless previously publicized.

provided in the citation, as shown in many of Mills's *Quicksheet* examples. Some researchers prefer citations with the test-takers named first. Following Mills's suggested format allows for clear and concise inclusion, at the end of the citation, of details that are not mentioned in the narrative.

The following sample citations are adapted from the format recommended in Mills's *Quicksheet*:

> "Family Finder," database report, *Family Tree DNA* (https://familytreedna.com/ : accessed 1 October 2014), for Tommy Curtis and Ira Smith, predicted 2nd-to-4th cousins; matches on chromosome 6 (start–stop points: 135113519–160850541), 33.63 cM, and chromosome 7 (start–stop points: 151306471–158850732), 11.58 cM; documented relationship 4th cousins.

> "Genome-wide comparison," database report, *23andMe* (https://23andme.com/ : accessed 1 October 2014), for Tommy Curtis and Ira Smith, predicted 3rd-to-4th cousins; matches on chromosome 6 (start–stop points: 135113519–160850541), 33.6 cM, and chromosome 7 (start–stop points: 151306471–158850732), 11.5 cM; documented relationship 4th cousins. Both tested with V3 microarray.

> "AncestryDNA Member Matches," database report, *AncestryDNA* (https://dna.ancestry.com/ : accessed 1 October 2014), for Tommy Curtis and Ira Smith, predicted 3rd cousins with 99% confidence; 97.554 cM shared across five segments; documented relationship 4th cousins.

> "Eurogenes K13 Admixture Proportions," database report, *GEDmatch* (http://gedmatch.com/ : accessed 1 October 2014), citing Eurogenes K13 model (rev 21 Nov 2013); for Tommy Curtis, kit no. T12345, predicting Amerindian segment on chromosome 11 (start–stop points: approximately 60M–68M).

> GEDmatch, "One-to-One DNA Comparison," database report, vers. 2, *GEDmatch* (http://v2.gedmatch.com/ : accessed 1 October 2014), kit nos. T12345 and T54321, 80.01 cM total; longest block on chromosome 6 (start–stop points: 135113519–160850541), 33.6 cM.

Proof Argument Elements and Process

The "Proof Arguments and Case Studies" chapter of *Professional Genealogy* explains how to structure and write a proof argument.[4] *Mastering Genealogical Proof* also covers how to structure a proof argument.[5] Publications of the Board for Certification of Genealogists (BCG) include many tips on writing proof arguments and forming a

---

[4] Elizabeth Shown Mills, "Proof Arguments and Case Studies," in Elizabeth Shown Mills, ed., *Professional Genealogy: A Manual for Researchers, Writers, Editors, Lecturers, and Librarians* (Baltimore, MD: Genealogical Publishing, 2001), 391–408.

[5] Jones, *Mastering Genealogical Proof*, 88–90.

focused research question.[6] The information in these publications applies to evidence in general. Specifics for incorporating DNA evidence are discussed in this chapter.

A proof discussion generally consists of a beginning, a middle, and an end:

- The beginning introduces the research question, states the hypothesis, discusses resources available to answer the question, and provides background context and details of prior research.
- The middle builds the case. It describes and interprets the evidence, addresses contradictory evidence (if any), and explains how the evidence leads to the conclusion.
- The end summarizes the evidence and context, and restates the hypothesis in a positive way.

The middle section is where the evidence, including DNA evidence, is presented. The most logical order of presentation is not necessarily that in which the evidence was found. Some conclusions are best supported by presenting evidence in a chronological manner (starting with the most recent records tracing back through older records, or starting with older records and following through to recent records), and some are best handled by presenting the strongest evidence first, followed by the weaker evidence. In situations where both documentary and DNA evidence support the conclusion, the discussion may be more understandable if documentary evidence is presented first, therein identifying descendants whose test results will be presented later. In some situations mingling the documentary and DNA evidence for each line works better, but this must be carefully structured so the reader is not confused.

When incorporating DNA evidence into a proof discussion, authors must consider how much biological background information should be provided to the reader. DNA inheritance patterns should be summarized, but only pertinent factors should be included. If the argument uses only one type of DNA test, background information on the other types may be omitted. Biological information must be explained concisely and simply so it can be understood by non-biologists.

Biological factors that affect the analysis of DNA evidence should be included. Are some of the Y-DNA STR markers considered fast-moving? Is an mtDNA difference in a known hot spot? Is a heteroplasmy involved? What is the size of a match on an atDNA segment? How many others in the family share the same marker differences or overlapping DNA segments?

---

[6] Laura DeGrazia, "Skillbuilding: Proof Arguments," *OnBoard* 15 (January 2009): 1–3; online, Board for Certification of Genealogists, *Skillbuilding: Proof Arguments* (http://www.bcgcertification.org/skill-builders/ skbld091.html). Barbara Vines Little, "Skillbuilding: It's Not That Hard to Write Proof Arguments," *OnBoard* 15 (September 2009): 20–23; online, Board for Certification of Genealogists, *Skillbuilding: It's Not that Hard to Write Proof Arguments* (http://www.bcgcertification.org/skillbuilders/skbld099.html). Harold Henderson, "Ten Minute Methodology: How to Ask Good Research Questions," *Board for Certification of Genealogists SpringBoard*, 28 January 2016 (http://bcgcertification.org/blog/2016/01/ten-minute-methodology-how-to-ask-good-research-questions/). For additional examples, see various articles in BCG's newsletter, *OnBoard*, and its blog, *SpringBoard*.

The depth and accuracy of the test-takers' family trees should be addressed. If a test-taker has many missing tree branches, the DNA analysis will be affected. Many other factors can also be considered in the discussion of DNA evidence.

Examples Incorporating DNA Evidence in Genealogical Writing

To learn how genetic genealogists incorporate DNA evidence into their proof arguments, it is helpful to read major genealogical journals. Journal articles illustrate the authors' methodology, analysis, explanations of the evidence (both traditional documentary evidence as well as DNA), and citations. Deconstructing others' analysis and writing is an excellent method to improve one's own skills.

The following recent examples of case studies and proof arguments combine documentary and DNA evidence to reach a genealogical conclusion:

- Fox, Judy Kellar. "Documents and DNA Identify a Little-Known Lee Family in Virginia." *National Genealogical Society Quarterly* 99 (June 2011): 85–96. [Incorporates Y-DNA evidence.]
- Hollister, Morna Lahnice. "Goggins and Goggans of South Carolina: DNA Helps Document the Basis of an Emancipated Family's Surname." *National Genealogical Society Quarterly* 102 (September 2014): 165–76. [Incorporates Y-DNA and atDNA evidence.]
- Jackson, B. Darrell. "George Craig of Howard County, Missouri: Genetic and Documentary Evidence of His Ancestry." *National Genealogical Society Quarterly* 99 (March 2011): 59–72. [Incorporates Y-DNA evidence.]
- Jones, Thomas W. "Too Few Sources to Solve a Family Mystery? Some Greenfields in Central and Western New York." *National Genealogical Society Quarterly* 103 (June 2015): 85–103. [Incorporates atDNA evidence.]
- Mills, Elizabeth Shown. "Testing the FAN Principle against DNA: Zilphy (Watts) Price Cooksey Cooksey of Georgia and Mississippi." *National Genealogical Society Quarterly* 102 (June 2014): 129–52. [Incorporates mtDNA and atDNA evidence.]

Chapter 8 Exercises

1. The following test-takers are identified as a match using the "One-to-One" tool at GEDmatch. Write a citation for this match.

      Test-taker 1: Kyle Lyons (GEDmatch kit A001234) (source: AncestryDNA)
      Test-taker 2: Ron Gough (GEDmatch kit M002345) (source: 23andMe)

      GEDmatch One-to-One matching segments (7 cM threshold):

Chromosome	Start	End	Centimorgans	SNPs
1	222127692	236160966	22.3	3,952
12	126612824	132276195	20.2	2,062

        Largest segment=22.3 cM
        Total of segments > 7 cM=42.5 cM
        Estimated number of generations to MRCA=4.4

2. Using the tables in question 7 of the "Incorporating DNA Testing in a Family Study" chapter, write a citation for the segments shared by Ira Smith (43) and Robert Smith (33).

3. Write a proof argument based on your own research or one of the exercises in this book. Use the *National Genealogical Society Quarterly* articles listed in this chapter as models. Form a study group with your peers, join a writing group, or ask a friend to critique your proof argument. After you feel comfortable with your writing,

consider submitting the article for possible publication in a local, state, regional, or national journal, or enter a genealogical writing contest. Lists of writing competitions can be found online.[7]

_____

_____

_____

---

[7] Kimberly Powell, "Genealogical Competitions, Scholarships & Contests," About.com, *Genealogy Education* (http://genealogy.about.com/od/education/tp/competitions.htm). Michael Hait, "Genealogy Writing Competitions," *Hait Family Research* (http://haitfamilyresearch.com/pdf_files/Genealogy Writing Competitions.pdf). Also see results from an Internet search for "genealogical writing contest."

CHAPTER 9

CONCLUSION

Genetic genealogy is a complex subject that can only be mastered with practice. To begin, the concepts in this book can be applied to confirm a known relationship. This will reinforce the techniques and understanding necessary to discover an unknown common ancestor with a DNA match. Researchers can become overwhelmed when faced with test results listing hundreds of people. Focusing on a small group of close matches (for example, several people who share one large, overlapping atDNA segment and who all have fairly robust family trees) will be more conducive to productive analysis. If progress stalls, the project can be placed on hold and focus shifted to another group. Eventually a conclusion will surface—a conclusion that may help resolve questions on the next project. New names on a match list may be newfound cousins with DNA that can answer a question.

This book addresses the basics of DNA analysis and correlation, with the goal of enabling beginning genetic genealogists to combine DNA findings with a family tree to reach a reasonable conclusion. It focuses on select topics to be discussed when asking others to take DNA tests and considerations for sharing DNA information with others. Lessons include different types of genealogically useful DNA tests and forming test plans to address focused researched questions. Incorporating multiple types of DNA into a family study and writing conclusions that include DNA evidence are discussed; also covered are the importance of thoroughly researched and well-documented trees, and ways that DNA evidence can extend a tree further back in time and confirm a tree's accuracy. Writing conclusions and having them reviewed by other genealogists will provide the best feedback. That feedback may come from colleagues, perhaps in a DNA Special Interest Group, or from journal editors.

There is still much to learn about the science of DNA and genetic genealogy applications. It is imperative that genealogists stay abreast of new developments. The "Reading and Source List" chapter includes information on blogs, forums, and mail lists, which are among the best places to learn about cutting-edge developments. The cited books, quick-reference guides, and articles provide information for self-study. Genetic genealogy tracks offered at institutes and by online venues provide instructor-led training. Courses at institutes are generally updated each year to incorporate new developments.

As knowledge of the science of DNA and genealogy applications grows, genetic genealogists may be better able to define criteria separating good matches from those that are less conclusive. New genetic genealogy tools will be developed to simplify some tasks. Being a thorough genetic genealogist requires a continuing investment in learning to analyze using the latest tools, techniques, and evaluation criteria.

APPENDIX A

CHARTS FOR EXERCISES

These charts represent families referenced in the exercises at the end of each chapter. Some charts are used for multiple chapters and multiple questions. It is advisable to make photocopies on which to work.

The charts are non-traditional in the sense that both persons comprising a couple are shown in one block. This is done to save space and fit more generations on the page. In these charts, the child listed first in a box is the descendant of the couple named in the box above. An "m." followed by a name represents a person's mate or spouse. Gender should be identifiable based on the given names.

Each question considers only the people shown on the chart. In actual situations, it is important to consider those lines not shown on the chart. Space does not allow inclusion of in-depth trees for every person named in an exercise, but in real-life scenarios the same analysis used to answer the exercise questions would have to be applied to the complete family trees of all persons involved in the research problem.

Descendants of John Ira Jones and Mary Ann (Smith) Jones

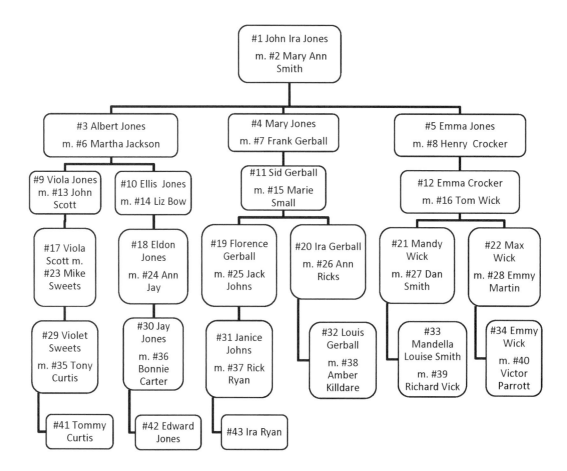

Descendants of Henry Smith

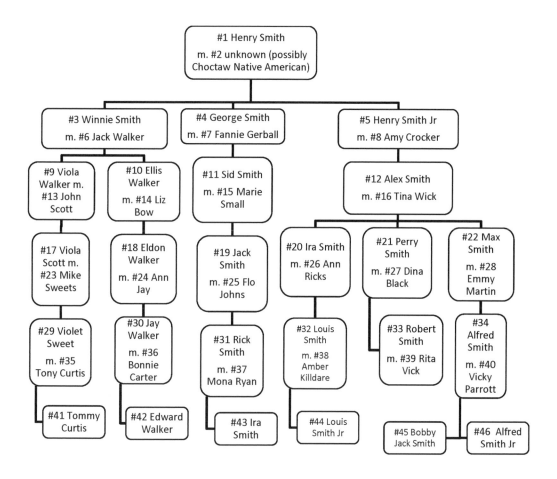

APPENDIX B

GLOSSARY

Some of the definitions included here are worded differently than in biological glossaries. The phrases were chosen to provide accurate definitions that are understandable by genealogists with no biological training.

admixture testing
The comparison of a person's DNA with a database of DNA from several known populations to identify ethnicity; the database samples that most closely match the person's DNA will be indicated, usually expressed as a percentage of DNA matching a specific population

algorithm
A process defining a mathematical calculation

allele
In biology, a variant of a gene; in genetic genealogy, the value of a marker tested by a testing company

ancestral SNP value
A SNP value that indicates a test-taker and his or her ancestors have either not mutated or have back-mutated at that location

atDNA
See *autosomal DNA*

autosomal DNA (atDNA)
Chromosomes 1 through 22, also called autosomes

back mutation
The result of two mutations, where a SNP mutates to a derived value, then mutates a second time to return to the ancestral value

base pair
The chemical bases (G, C, A, or T) found on one rung of the DNA ladder

bio-geographical analysis
See *admixture testing*

Cambridge Reference Sequence/revised Cambridge Reference Sequence (CRS/rCRS)
The traditional reference sequence to which mtDNA test results are compared; the CRS/rCRS was the first full mtDNA sequenced and was the only sequence available for comparisons until construction of the RSRS in 2012

centimorgan (cM)
A relative segment-length that incorporates the statistical probability of a segment being separated during recombination (as opposed to Megabase (Mb), which is a physical length); 1 cM is equivalent to a 1 percent (one in one hundred) chance that a DNA segment will recombine within one generation; on average 1 cM is equivalent to about one million base pairs, although this varies by location and sex

chromosome
A very long double-helix of DNA found in the nucleus of a cell and organized with proteins; humans have twenty-two pairs of autosomal chromosomes and one pair of sex chromosomes

chromosome browser
A tool that creates a graphical image or table of atDNA or X-DNA that is shared by two or more test-takers

chromosome map
A graphical display of chromosome segments mapped to one or more ancestors or ancestral couples

clade
A group consisting of a common ancestor and all lineal descendants; a single branch on the mtDNA or Y-DNA tree

cM
See *centimorgan*

coding region (CR)
The segment of the mtDNA molecule that contains the code for genes

comma separated values (CSV)
A standard computer-file format used for data interchange; CSV files are typically read using a spreadsheet program or a plain text editor, and are incapable of retaining some data formatting

control region
The segment of the mtDNA molecule that does not contain the code for genes; see also *hyper-variable region/hyper-variable segment*

crossover, crossing over
See *recombination*

CR
See *coding region*

CRS/rCRS
See *Cambridge Reference Sequence/revised Cambridge Reference Sequence*

CSV
See *comma separated values*

deoxyribonucleic acid (DNA)
The biological matter that carries genetic information

derived SNP value
A SNP value that indicates the SNP has mutated from the ancestral SNP value

DNA
See *deoxyribonucleic acid*

DNA match
A person who is on a match list of a focus person, indicating matching DNA segments or markers; or, a segment of DNA shared by two or more people

download
The act of copying data from an external website to one's own device

DYS
DNA Y-chromosome segment

endogamy
The practice of individuals marrying within the same group over a long period of time; examples include Acadians, the Amish, Ashkenazi Jews, people from Newfoundland, island groups, and other isolated settlements

ethnicity testing
See *admixture testing*

family SNP
Relatively recent mutations that only propagated within the past few hundred years

FASTA
A text-format file where the first line describes and comments on the sequence and the rest of the file consists of letters representing nucleotides; a FASTA file contains raw data for mtDNA

FIR
See *fully-identical region*

FMS
See *full mitochondrial sequence*

full mitochondrial sequence (FMS)
Sequence of the entire mtDNA genome, including the hyper-variable region and the coding region

fully-identical region (FIR)
A DNA segment where two siblings inherited matching DNA from both parents; or

where two cousins share DNA on both sides of the family at the same location; compare to *half-identical region*

GEDCOM
An abbreviation for Genealogical Data Communication, a standardized format for packaging electronic genealogical data, usually a family tree

Genealogical Proof Standard (GPS)
A standard used by genealogists to evaluate the strength of a genealogical assertion; its five criteria call for reasonably exhaustive research, sound documentation, skilled analysis and correlation of information and evidence, resolution of any conflicting evidence, and a clearly written discussion of the evidence and the reasoning

genealogical timeframe
The period of time that can be documented genealogically using historical records

genealogical tree
A tree of all an individual's ancestors

genetic distance
A measure of genetic divergence or similarity between two test-takers

genetic genealogy
The application of DNA evidence to answer a genealogical question

Genetic Genealogy Standards
Standards for incorporating genetic genealogy into genealogical research; see the Genetic Genealogy Standards website (http://www.geneticgenealogystandards.com/)

genetic network
A linked group of three or more individuals who share DNA; the DNA segments may be shared by as few as two or as many as all members of the group

genetic tree
A tree of an individual's ancestors who contributed to that individual's DNA; a subset of an individual's genealogical tree

genotype
The DNA value for a tested marker; genotype is often used as the column heading in genetic genealogy reports that display the allele or chemical value of a specific DNA location

GPS
See *Genealogical Proof Standard*

half-identical region (HIR)
A DNA segment where two siblings inherited matching DNA from only one parent and inherited differing segments of DNA from the other parent; or a DNA

segment shared by two cousins who only share DNA on one chromosome at that location; compare to *fully-identical region*

haplogroup
A name given to a large branch of the human genetic tree; there are separate genetic trees for Y-DNA and for mtDNA; two individuals must have the same haplogroup to be closely related on the Y-DNA or mtDNA line

haplotype
A set of two or more DNA-marker values carried by a person or organism

heteroplasmy
The presence of more than one mtDNA sequence in a cell or individual, as in where mtDNA has mutated and both the original and the mutated sequence can be detected in the individual

HIR
See *half-identical region*

HVR/HVS
See *hyper-variable region/hyper-variable segment*

hyper-variable region/hyper-variable segment (HVR/HVS)
A segment of mtDNA, not part of the coding region, in which changes or mutations are frequently seen

IBC
See *identical by coincidence*

IBD
See *identical by descent*

IBS
See *identical by state*

ICW
See *in common with*

identical by coincidence (IBC)
A term used to describe a false positive in which two people appear to have matching DNA segments due to limitations of current testing procedures, algorithms used for comparisons, or both

identical by descent (IBD)
A term used to describe two people who have matching DNA segments inherited from a common ancestor

identical by state (IBS)
A term used to describe two people who have matching DNA segments due to common ancestral populations

in common with (ICW)
A list of DNA test-takers who share DNA (have DNA "in common with") a person; the shared DNA can be on any chromosome and is not necessarily on the same segment for everyone on the ICW list

indels
Insertions or deletions of base pairs; often discussed in relation to mtDNA, but applicable to all types of DNA

inheritance pattern
The path through ancestors by which a particular type of DNA may have been inherited

International Society of Genetic Genealogists (ISOGG)
An organization whose mission is to "advocate for and educate about the use of genetics as a tool for genealogical research while promoting a supportive network for genetic genealogists"; see the ISOGG website (http://isogg.org/) and the *ISOGG Wiki* (http://isogg.org/wiki/)

ISOGG
See *International Society of Genetic Genealogists*

marker
A named DNA segment, STR, or SNP at a defined location

match list
A list of people in a company or third-party database who share DNA with a focus person

matching segment
A tested DNA segment that matches segments belonging to one or more other test-takers

matrilineal line
The line of inheritance through which mtDNA passes; the line from a person to his or her mother, to her mother (the maternal grandmother), to her mother, and so on

Mb/Mbp
See *megabase/megabase pairs*

megabase/megabase pairs (Mb/Mbp)
One million base pairs; a physical length of DNA, as opposed to cM, which is a relative length of DNA

meiosis
A specialized cell division that creates eggs and sperm for reproduction; compare to *mitosis*

misattributed parentage
A term used to describe a scenario where the biological parent is not the expected or documented parent; also referred to as a *non-paternal event*

miscall
An allele that is incorrectly identified due to an error while sequencing the DNA

mitochondrial DNA (mtDNA)
DNA carried outside of the nucleus of a human cell and passed from a mother to all of her children; males inherit mtDNA from their mothers but do not pass it to their children, while females inherit mtDNA from their mothers and pass it to their male and female children

mitosis
Cell division that results in two identical copies of the cell; compare to *meiosis*

most recent common ancestor (MRCA)
The most recent ancestor shared by two or more persons

MRCA
See *most recent common ancestor*

mtDNA
See *mitochondrial DNA*

mutation
A change in the DNA chemical or the number of repeats at a particular location or marker, most often due to an error when DNA is copied

no call
An allele that cannot be read while sequencing the DNA; typically identified as "- -" (hyphen hyphen) in raw data

non-paternal event (NPE)
A term used to describe a scenario where the biological parent is not the expected or documented parent; also referred to as *misattributed parentage*, which is the preferred terminology

NPE
See *non-paternal event*

nucleotide
The basic structural unit of DNA

overlapping segment
A block of DNA with start or stop locations that appear to encompass or overlap a DNA segment of a matching person; one segment may be the same size or longer than the other, but at least a portion of the segments overlap

patrilineal line
The line of inheritance through which Y-DNA passes; the line from a man to his father, to his father (the paternal grandfather), to his father, and so on

phasing
The process of determining which of two alleles was inherited from one parent

private SNP
See *family SNP*

pseudo-segment
A segment of DNA that is falsely identified as being shared; alleles inherited from the maternal and paternal chromosome are strung together, making it incorrectly appear as if the DNA of two test-takers matches

raw data
For atDNA, a file containing a list of the allele values or DNA chemicals (A, C, G, or T) on both chromosomes at each tested location; for mtDNA, the values contained in a FASTA file that represent the DNA chemicals detected at each location tested; for Y-STR tests, the marker name and value of the marker (the number of repeats at that location); for Y-SNP tests, the marker name and whether the SNP is ancestral (not mutated, sometimes represented by a hyphen or minus sign) or derived (mutated, sometimes represented as a plus sign); some data file formats also indicate the quality of the sequenced data, the DNA chemical detected at each location, or both

rCRS
See *Cambridge Reference Sequence/revised Cambridge Reference Sequence*

recombination
The process in which segments of DNA inherited from a person's parents are exchanged, creating unique chromosomes to be passed to the next generation in the sperm or egg

Reconstructed Sapiens Reference Sequence (RSRS)
A reference sequence reconstructed in 2012 to which mtDNA test results are compared; a comparison to the RSRS lists all mtDNA mutations of a person as compared to Mitochondrial Eve, the matrilineal-line ancestor of all humans living today

reference SNP identification (RSID)
The name of a marker or DNA location

reversion
See *back mutation*

Revised Cambridge Reference Sequence (rCRS)
See *Cambridge Reference Sequence/revised Cambridge Reference Sequence*

RSID
See *Reference SNP identification*

RSRS
See *Reconstructed Sapiens Reference Sequence*

segment
A block of DNA; a consecutive section of DNA from one chromosome

segment data
A detailed list of DNA shared by two test-takers stating (for each matching segment) the chromosome number, start location, ending location, and some additional information

sex chromosomes
The chromosomes that determine gender; the X and Y chromosomes; females have two X chromosomes; males have one X chromosome and one Y chromosome

short tandem repeat (STR)
A short, repeating pattern of DNA at consecutive rungs of the DNA ladder

significant segment size
The minimum size a shared DNA segment must be to be considered meaningful to analysis; genetic genealogists differ with respect to practical minimums; minimum segment sizes of 5, 7, 10, and 20 cM are commonly used for atDNA and X-DNA analysis

single nucleotide polymorphism (SNP)
The base pair found at one rung of the DNA ladder; a SNP value can vary from one person to another

SNP
See *single nucleotide polymorphism*

STR
See *short tandem repeat*

sub-clade
A sub-group of a clade; a sub-branch of the mtDNA or Y-DNA human tree

terminal SNP
The Y-SNP that defines the most distant branch of the human family tree for which a test-taker has tested

TG
See *triangulated group*

threshold
The amount of DNA two test-takers must share before a testing company or third-party tool includes them on each other's match lists (the company or tool comparison threshold); when discussing size of shared atDNA blocks, threshold may indicate the smallest segment a researcher considers (for example, blocks smaller than 5, 7, 10, or 20 cM in size are not used in analysis, as many of the smaller blocks are false positives, IBS, or IBC)

triangulated group (TG)
A group of test-takers who match each other along the same or an overlapping segment of the same chromosome; because each person has one copy of each chromosome from the mother and one from the father, two triangulated groups can exist for each segment of each chromosome; one of those groups should share maternal ancestry, while the other shares paternal ancestry

triangulation
The process of comparing DNA segments from three or more people to verify they all share DNA along the same or an overlapping segment of a particular chromosome, thereby forming a triangulated group (TG); shared DNA segments of a significant size indicate all may have inherited that DNA segment from a common ancestor

uniparental
The transmission of DNA from just one parent; transmission of Y-DNA along the patrilineal line is an example of uniparental transmission, as is the transmission of mtDNA along the matrilineal line

upload
The act of copying data from a personal device to an external website

X-DNA
DNA on the X chromosome; a woman inherits one X chromosome from her mother and one X chromosome from her father; a man inherits one X chromosome from his mother and none from his father

Y-DNA
DNA on the Y chromosome; a woman does not inherit Y-DNA; a man inherits one Y chromosome from his father and none from his mother

Y-SNP
A SNP on the Y chromosome

Y-STR
An STR on the Y chromosome

zygote
A fertilized ovum (egg); a cell containing two complete sets of chromosomes resulting from the fusion of two cells, each of which contains one unpaired set of chromosomes

Additional terms are defined in these two glossaries:

"Genetics Glossary." *ISOGG Wiki.* http://www.isogg.org/wiki/Genetics_Glossary.

"Glossary of Genetic Terms 2016." *ISOGG.*
http://www.isogg.org/tree/ISOGG_Glossary.html.

APPENDIX C

READING AND SOURCE LIST

Blogs and Online Lessons

23andMe. *23andMe Blog*.
    http://blog.23andme.com/.

Aulicino, Emily. *DNA-Genealem's Genetic Genealogy*.
    http://genealem-geneticgenealogy.blogspot.com/.

Bartlett, Jim. *Segment-ology*.
    https://segmentology.org/.

Bettinger, Blaine. *The Genetic Genealogist*.
    http://www.thegeneticgenealogist.com/.

Christmas, Shannon. *Through the Trees*.
    http://throughthetreesblog.tumblr.com/.

Dowell, David R. *Dr D Digs Up Ancestors*.
    http://blog.ddowell.com/.

Estes, Roberta. *DNAeXplained—Genetic Genealogy*.
    https://dna-explained.com/.

Family Tree DNA. *Family Tree DNA Learning Center—News*.
    https://www.familytreedna.com/learn/topics/news/.

ISOGG. "Genetic genealogy blogs." *ISOGG Wiki*.
    http://www.isogg.org/wiki/Genetic_genealogy_blogs.

Kennett, Debbie. *Cruwys News*. http://cruwys.blogspot.com/.

Lacopo, Michael. *Hoosier Daddy*.
    http://roots4u.blogspot.com/.

Moore, CeCe. *Your Genetic Genealogist*.
    http://www.yourgeneticgenealogist.com/.

Owston, Jim. *The Lineal Arboretum*.
    http://linealarboretum.blogspot.com/.

Perkins, Steven. *On-line Journal of Genetics and Genealogy*.
    http://jgg-online.blogspot.com/.

Russell, Judy G. *The Legal Genealogist*.
    http://www.legalgenealogist.com/.

Walker, Rebecca. *Solving Genealogy Puzzles with DNA*.
    http://genealogypuzzlesdna.blogspot.com/.

Wayne, Debbie Parker. *Deb's Delvings in Genealogy*.
    http://debsdelvings.blogspot.com/.

Wheaton, Kelly. *Beginner's Guide to Genetic Genealogy.*
    https://sites.google.com/site/wheatonsurname/beginners-guide-to-genetic-ge-
    nealogy/.

Books, Quick-Reference Guides, and Articles on Genetic Genealogy

Aulicino, Emily D. *Genetic Genealogy: The Basics and Beyond.* Bloomington, IN: Au-
    thorHouse, 2014.

Bettinger, Blaine. [Multiple articles.] *Association of Professional Genealogists Quarterly*
    30, no. 2 (June 2015)–present.

————and Matt Dexter. *I Have the Results of My Genetic Genealogy Test, Now What?*
    N.p.: Bettinger and Dexter, 2008. *Family Tree DNA.*
    http://www.familytreedna.com/pdf-docs/Interpreting-Genetic-Genealogy-Re-
    sults_web_optimized.pdf.

Dowell, David R. *NextGen Genealogy: The DNA Connection.* Santa Barbara, CA:
    Libraries Unlimited, 2015.

Fitzpatrick, Colleen. *Forensic Genealogy.* Revised Edition. Fountain Valley, CA: Rice
    Book Press, 2013.

————and Andrew Yeiser. *DNA and Genealogy.* Fountain Valley, CA: Rice Book
    Press, 2005.

Fox, Judy Kellar. "Documents and DNA Identify a Little-Known Lee Family in Virginia."
    National Genealogical Society Quarterly 99 (June 2011): 85–96. [Incorporates
    Y-DNA evidence.]

"Genetics and Genealogy." Special issue, *National Genealogical Society Quarterly* 93,
    no. 4 (December 2005).

Hill, Richard. *Finding Family: My Search for Roots and the Secrets in My DNA.* N.p.:
    Hill, 2012.

————. *Guide to DNA Testing: How to Identify Ancestors, Confirm Relationships, and
    Measure Ethnic Ancestry through DNA Testing.* Kindle edition. N.p.: Hill, 2014.

Hollister, Morna Lahnice. "Goggins and Goggans of South Carolina: DNA Helps Docu-
    ment the Basis of an Emancipated Family's Surname." *National Genealogical
    Society Quarterly* 102 (September 2014): 165–76. [Incorporates Y-DNA and
    atDNA evidence.]

Jackson, B. Darrell. "George Craig of Howard County, Missouri: Genetic and Docu-
    mentary Evidence of His Ancestry." *National Genealogical Society Quarterly* 99
    (March 2011): 59–72. [Incorporates Y-DNA evidence.]

Jones, Thomas W. "Too Few Sources to Solve a Family Mystery? Some Greenfields in
    Central and Western New York." *National Genealogical Society Quarterly* 103
    (June 2015): 85–103. [Incorporates atDNA evidence.]

Kennett, Debbie. *DNA and Social Networking: A Guide to Genealogy in the Twenty-First Century*. Stroud, Gloucestershire, UK: History Press, 2011.

Mills, Elizabeth Shown. "Testing the FAN Principle against DNA: Zilphy (Watts) Price Cooksey Cooksey of Georgia and Mississippi." *National Genealogical Society Quarterly* 102 (June 2014): 129–52. [Incorporates mtDNA and atDNA evidence.]

———. *Quicksheet: Citing Genetic Sources for History Research, Evidence Style*. Baltimore, MD: Genealogical Publishing, 2015.

Pomery, Chris. *DNA and Family History: How Genetic Testing Can Advance Your Genealogical Research*. Toronto, ON: Dundurn Group, 2006.

———. *Family History in the Genes: Trace Your DNA and Grow Your Family Tree*. Kew, Surrey: The National Archives, 2007.

Shawker, Thomas H. *Unlocking Your Genetic History*. Nashville, TN.: Rutledge Hill Press, 2004.

Smolenyak, Megan Smolenyak and Ann Turner. *Trace Your Roots with DNA*. Emmaus, PA: Rodale, 2004.

Southard, Diahan. *Getting Started: Genetics for the Genealogist*. DNA Quick Guides. N.p. Genealogy Gems Publications, 2014.

———. *Y Chromosome DNA for the Genealogist*. DNA Quick Guides. N.p. Genealogy Gems Publications, 2014.

———. *Mitochondrial DNA for the Genealogist*. DNA Quick Guides. N.p. Genealogy Gems Publications, 2014.

———. *Autosomal DNA for the Genealogist*. DNA Quick Guides. N.p. Genealogy Gems Publications, 2014.

———. *Understanding AncestryDNA: A Companion Guide to Autosomal DNA for the Genealogist*. DNA Quick Guides. N.p. Genealogy Gems Publications, 2015.

———. *Understanding Family Tree DNA: A Companion Guide to Autosomal DNA for the Genealogist*. DNA Quick Guides. N.p. Genealogy Gems Publications, 2015.

———. *Understanding 23andMe: A Companion Guide to Autosomal DNA for the Genealogist*. DNA Quick Guides. N.p. Genealogy Gems Publications, 2015.

Wayne, Debbie Parker. [Multiple articles.] *Association of Professional Genealogists Quarterly* 29, no. 1 (March 2014)–30, no. 1 (March 2015).

———. Genetic Genealogy Journey. *NGS Magazine* 39, no. 3 (October/November/December 2013)–present.

For additional book titles, see "Genetic genealogy books." *ISOGG Wiki*. http://www.isogg.org/wiki/Genetic_genealogy_books.

Glossaries

"Genetics Glossary." *ISOGG Wiki.*
     http://www.isogg.org/wiki/Genetics_Glossary.

"Glossary of Genetic Terms–2016." *ISOGG.*
     http://www.isogg.org/tree/ISOGG_Glossary.html.

Lists, Groups, FAQs, and Forums

DNA: Autosomal-DNA. Discussion list.
     http://lists.rootsweb.ancestry.com/index/other/DNA/AUTOSOMAL-DNA.html.

DNA: Genealogy-DNA. Discussion list.
     http://lists.rootsweb.com/index/other/DNA/GENEALOGY-DNA.html.

DNA-Newbie. Discussion list.
     http://groups.yahoo.com/group/DNA-NEWBIE/.

Family Tree DNA. *Family Tree DNA Forums.*
     http://forums.familytreedna.com/.

Family Tree DNA. *Family Tree DNA Learning Center.*
     http://www.familytreedna.com/learn/.

There are also many lists related to DNA research on specific surnames, DNA
     signatures, ethnic groups, and localities.

Genetic Genealogy Training

Family Tree University.
     https://www.familytreeuniversity.com/.

Genealogical Research Institute of Pittsburgh (GRIP).
     http://www.gripitt.org/.

Institute of Genealogy and Historical Research (IGHR). http://ighr.samford.edu/.
     [Beginning in 2017, IGHR will be held at the Georgia Center for Continuing
     Education on the Athens, Georgia, campus of the University of Georgia.
     Use a search engine to find the new website if Samford no longer provides a
     forward link.]

National Genealogical Society.
     http://www.ngsgenealogy.org/.

Salt Lake Institute of Genealogy (SLIG).
     http://www.infouga.org/. [Click on SLIG in the menu to the left.]

University of Strathclyde.
   http://www.strath.ac.uk/.

Virtual Institute of Genealogical Research.
   http://vigrgenealogy.com/.

Genealogical Research

Every issue of the *National Genealogical Society Quarterly* includes articles demon-
   strating use of the Genealogical Proof Standard, methodology and inclusion of
   historical context.
   http://www.ngsgenealogy.org/.

Board for Certification of Genealogists. *Genealogy Standards*. 50th anniversary edition.
   Nashville, TN: Ancestry Imprint, Turner Publishing, 2014.

Greenwood, Val D. *The Researcher's Guide to American Genealogy*. 3rd edition.
   Baltimore, MD: Genealogical Publishing, 2000.

Jones, Thomas W. *Mastering Genealogical Proof*. Arlington, VA: National Genealogical
   Society, 2013.

Leary, Helen F. M. *North Carolina Research: Genealogy and Local History*. 2nd
   edition. Raleigh, NC: North Carolina Genealogical Society, 1996.

Merriman, Brenda Dougall. *Genealogical Standards of Evidence: A Guide for Family
   Historians*. Toronto, ON: Ontario Genealogical Society, 2010.

Mills, Elizabeth Shown. *Evidence Explained: Citing History Sources from Artifacts to
   Cyberspace*. 3rd edition. Baltimore, MD: Genealogical Publishing, 2015.

———. *Evidence Explained: Historical Analysis, Citation & Source Usage*.
   https://www.evidenceexplained.com/.

———, ed. *Professional Genealogy : A Manual for Researchers, Writers, Editors,
   Lecturers, and Librarians*. Baltimore, MD: Genealogical Publishing, 2001.

Rose, Christine. *Genealogical Proof Standard: Building a Solid Case*. 4th edition
   revised. San Jose, CA: CR Publications, 2014.

Szucs, Loretto Dennis, and Sandra Hargreave Luebking, eds. *The Source: A Guidebook
   of American Genealogy*. 3rd edition. Provo, UT: Ancestry Publishing, 2006.
   Ancestry.com Wiki.
   http://www.ancestry.com/wiki/index.php?title=The_Source:_A_Guidebook_to_
   American_Genealogy : 2010.

APPENDIX D

EXERCISE ANSWERS

Chapter 2 Exercise Answers

1. The goal is to determine when Isaac Ryan first bought land in what is now Jackson County, Mississippi. Can DNA evidence help achieve this goal? If so, how?

   No. This is not a question where DNA evidence is likely to be helpful. This question could best be answered by researching land, deed, and tax records.

2. The goal is to determine whether the Isaac Ryan who first bought land in 1798 in what is now Jackson County, Mississippi, is the ancestor of Jonathan Ryan. Can DNA evidence help achieve this goal? If so, how?

   Yes, if there are living descendants in the correct lines who agree to be tested. Assume we have proven our Jonathan Ryan line back to a male we believe is the son of the Isaac Ryan who first bought land in 1798 in what is now Jackson County, Mississippi. By researching all lines of descent from this Isaac Ryan we may find living cousins descended from other children of Isaac. If our line and one of the other lines follow the patrilineal line (father to son to grandson to great-grandson and so on), we may be able to use Y-DNA to link our line to the other son's line. If the line of a descendant passes through both sons and daughters, Y-DNA would not be useful, but atDNA may show links between the cousins.

3. Nathan suspects that Ethan Kilgore disinherited his sons Hugh and Philip just before his death in 1861 because, according to family legend, Ethan's wife informed him in a fit of rage that they weren't actually his children. Instead, the legend goes, they were the children of a former neighbor called Simon or Samuel Smith. Research in census records reveals a Samuel Simons living next door in 1820 and 1830, years that bookend the decade during which Hugh and Philip were born. Can DNA evidence be utilized to examine the question of why Ethan Kilgore disinherited his sons?

   Possibly, although not directly. If Hugh and Philip have descendants, testing Y-DNA or atDNA may provide evidence to answer whether Hugh and Philip are children of Ethan Kilgore or Samuel Simons. For example, Y-DNA and atDNA of Hugh and Philip's descendants could be compared to the Y-DNA and atDNA of another of Ethan Kilgore's descendants (or a descendant of one of Ethan Kilgore's ancestors) and to a descendant of Samuel Simons. DNA evidence suggesting they are children of Ethan Kilgore may not shed any light on why

Ethan disinherited them, but if the DNA evidence suggests they are children of Samuel Simons or some other person, the findings may indirectly support the family story.

Henry is a professional genealogist and has been hired by Charles DuMond to research his DuMond line. Charles suspects his grandfather William DuMond was born William Rivers, but he has been unable to prove the name change. Charles has asked Henry to find evidence to support or refute the Rivers surname hypothesis. Using this scenario, answer questions 4 and 5.

4. Henry has been a professional genealogist for twenty-five years and is well versed in every record type that could be used for this project. However Henry is skeptical of DNA testing and has never utilized or explored it in his own or his clients' research. Can Henry's research satisfy the GPS for this project if he intentionally doesn't consider DNA because he doesn't believe it is accurate?

   Most likely not. It is impossible to satisfy the GPS in a scenario where a known record type is potentially available but is intentionally being ignored despite there being no reasonable basis to question its validity. In this case, Y-DNA and atDNA test results are key pieces of evidence that are almost certain to shed light on the genealogical question. Since they are not being considered, the GPS element of reasonably exhaustive research is not satisfied. Henry should either educate himself about DNA (on his own time or with the permission of the client), ask for assistance from another genealogist knowledgeable about DNA, or inform his client that he is unable to fully complete this project.

5. Henry decides to inform his client that Y-DNA or atDNA testing could potentially shed light on the question, but that he is not educated on the subject. Henry suggests that he or the client contact another genealogist who is well versed in the use of DNA. The client informs Henry that he isn't interested in that option. Can Henry complete the assigned project with any confidence, and can the project satisfy the GPS?

   Henry can complete the assigned project with confidence. Effectively, the client is asking Henry to complete all available research, but to omit DNA evidence. Henry appears to be more than capable of completing this project. Clients are free to ask genealogists to perform any research, ranging from a very simple index look-up to the re-creation of a complex, multi-generational family tree. Clients are also free to limit a project to, for example, certain record types, hours, and repositories.

   Client-imposed limitations may mean that reasonably exhaustive research cannot be conducted. Here, for example, the client-imposed limitation means that a record type almost guaranteed to be informative is not being considered. Accordingly, Henry's current project cannot satisfy the GPS, but it can provide an answer to Mr. DuMond's research question—namely, whether all available evidence, minus DNA evidence, supports or refutes the hypothesis that William DuMond was born William Rivers.

Genealogist Julianna Turner has researched the Wilcox family in and around Jonesborough, Tennessee, for the past two decades. Based on the documentary evidence, she hypothesizes that Benjamin Wilcox is the father of the three males responsible for the three main Wilcox families in the region. Julianna would like to conduct Y-DNA testing on the three Wilcox lines to support or reject her hypothesis. Although there is the possibility that atDNA might shed light on the question, at the time being she is only considering Y-DNA. Using this scenario, answer questions 6 and 7.

6. After extensive research Julianna discovers that the first Wilcox family, descended from Thomas Wilcox, has thousands of descendants but no direct line male descendants. If Y-DNA testing of the Thomas Wilcox line is impossible, and atDNA testing is not possible for various other reasons, can Julianna's research satisfy the GPS when analyzing whether Thomas Wilcox was the son of Benjamin Wilcox?

   Yes, even though she cannot access a particular record type, it is still possible for Julianna's research to meet the GPS. She can still perform reasonably exhaustive research, resolve any conflicts, and reach a conclusion based on all the evidence she is able to identify. As part of her research, she recognizes that DNA testing could help support or refute her genealogical hypothesis, but is foreclosed from pursuing DNA testing for reasons beyond her control. The complete lack of a record—because the record never existed, because it existed but was later destroyed, or because it is legally or ethically inaccessible—does not prevent a genealogist from meeting the GPS.

7. Some years later, Julianna learns that before he died the last man with Thomas Wilcox's Y-DNA had a son that the family didn't know about. This living son is in fact the last known male with Thomas Wilcox's Y-DNA. When Julianna contacts him, he refuses to undergo any type of DNA testing. If DNA testing of the Thomas Wilcox line is possible but cannot be performed due to refusal by the last living direct-line male, can Julianna's research satisfy the GPS when analyzing whether Thomas Wilcox was the son of Benjamin Wilcox?

   Yes, even though she cannot access a particular record type, it is still possible for Julianna's research to meet the GPS. Once again, Julianna is prevented from pursuing DNA testing for reasons beyond her control. The record exists, but the holder of that record has declined to share it and is under no obligation to share it. The scenario where a record exists but is completely inaccessible is effectively no different than a scenario where a record does not exist.

8. Brenda is working on a Kinship Determination Project (KDP) for submission in her BCG application portfolio. A KDP is a narrative genealogy, lineage, or pedigree that documents at least three ancestral generations. Like other genealogical proofs, a KDP requires that "the underlying research [is] reasonably thorough" and that Brenda consult "all sources and information items that competent genealogists would use to

support the conclusion."[1] Brenda's KDP is based on her paternal grandfather's family. Her research has revealed that her great-grandfather Ronald was the product of a widely known but mostly undocumented non-paternal event; all the available evidence points to a single man as the biological father. Her own atDNA testing has proven largely inconclusive, despite testing herself and numerous third and fourth cousins. Y-DNA testing may be the final piece of evidence needed to confidently conclude the identity of Ronald's father. Brenda's father—Ronald's grandson—is still living and is the last person available for the Y-DNA test. He has advanced Alzheimer's disease and doesn't recognize Brenda. Although Brenda's father's legal representative has signed off on the DNA tests without reservation, Brenda has decided that it would be unethical to test her father. Instead she submits the KDP without any Y-DNA evidence, even though it is technically available to her. Can her KDP satisfy the GPS, or has she failed to conduct thorough research that considers all sources?

> *Yes, Brenda's KDP can satisfy the GPS despite her decision to forego the Y-DNA testing. No element of the GPS requires that a genealogist violate a reasonable ethical standpoint in order to obtain a record. Although Brenda is legally authorized to access the record, she has decided that a legal representative's authorization is not sufficient and that her father is incapable of providing his own authorization.*

9. Sadly, Brenda's father passes away before she submits her KDP. The Genetic Genealogy Standards provide that "in the case of a deceased individual, consent can be obtained from a legal representative."[2] The legal representative authorizes a Y-DNA test at the request of Brenda's sister, Rachel. Rachel receives the results and offers to share them with Brenda. However, Brenda has reservations about using the results without her father's explicit authorization, and submits her KDP without any Y-DNA evidence. Can her KDP satisfy the GPS, or has she failed to conduct thorough research that considers all sources?

> *The answer to this question is less clear. On the one hand, Brenda's father did not give consent himself and Brenda may have a reason she doesn't want to view her father's test results without his explicit permission. On the other hand, Brenda's father is deceased and therefore does not have a right of privacy, and the Y-DNA test results were legally and arguably ethically obtained.*

---

[1] Board for Certification of Genealogists, *Genealogy Standards*, 31 (Standard 51).
[2] *Genetic Genealogy Standards*, Standard 2.

Chapter 3 Exercise Answers

Use the family tree chart titled "Descendants of Thomas and Sarah (Underhill) Chrisman" to answer questions 1, 2, and 3. The genealogist has confirmed that there are no known common ancestors for the people on the chart other than those shown. Each kinship link has been confirmed with strong documentary evidence.

Hint: The easiest way to answer these questions is to make a copy of the chart, then, beginning with Thomas Chrisman, use a unique mark to identify all descendants who may have inherited Y-DNA from him.

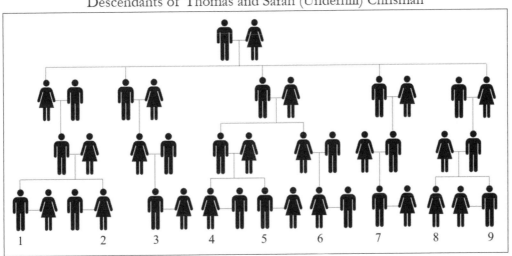

Descendants of Thomas and Sarah (Underhill) Chrisman

1. Which of the descendants in the bottom row (the great-grandchildren) may have inherited the Y-DNA of their great-grandfather Thomas Chrisman?

    Only great-grandchildren numbered 5 and 7 should possess the great-grandfather's Y-DNA. There is a female located in the family tree between each of the other male great-grandchildren (numbers 1, 3, and 9) and their great-grandfather, which interrupts the Y-DNA line. Males numbered 1, 3, and 9 will possess Y-DNA from their own paternal great-grandfathers, who aren't shown on this chart.

2. How many men in the family tree may have inherited their Y-DNA from Thomas Chrisman? Do not include Thomas in the count.

    A total of seven of the men (not including Thomas) in the family tree should have inherited their Y-DNA from Thomas Underhill.

Descendants of Thomas and Sarah (Underhill) Chrisman

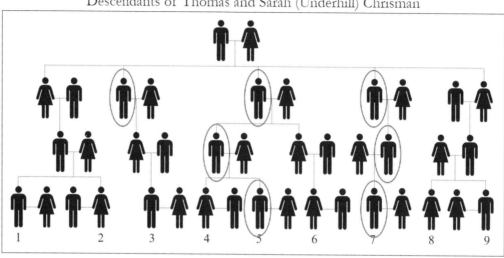

3. Thomas Chrisman had three sons, each of whom has grandsons of his own. Is there a grandson in each of the three sons' lines who may have inherited Thomas Chrisman's Y-DNA? Why or why not?

> *Even though all three sons have male grandchildren, they do not each have a grandchild who may have inherited their Y-DNA. The oldest son has a male grandchild (3) who is the son of his daughter, and thus the Y-DNA line was interrupted. The oldest son's Y-DNA line has "daughtered out."*

Use the family tree chart titled "Descendants of Lawrence and Diana (?) Richmond" to answer questions 4 and 5.

Descendants of Lawrence and Diana (?) Richmond

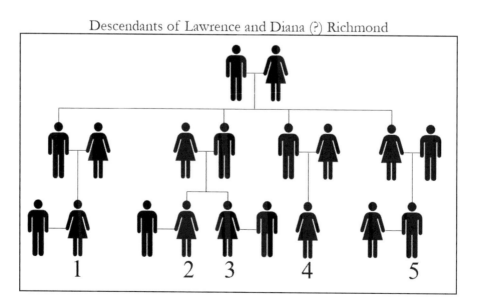

4. Which of the five grandchildren in this chart (numbered 1 through 5) may have inherited their Y-DNA from their grandfather Lawrence Richmond?

None of the grandchildren should possess the grandfather's Y-DNA. Grandchild 5, the only male, is a child of the grandfather's daughter. He could not have received his Y-DNA from his maternal grandfather. If the grandchildren are the only living descendants of the grandfather, then his Y-DNA has "daughtered out."

5. Based on the answer to question 4, what is the next step in examining the Y-DNA of grandfather Lawrence Richmond?

The next step is to research Lawrence Richmond's family to determine whether Lawrence had any brothers who passed the Richmond family Y-DNA to a living male willing to take a Y-DNA test. If not, research should investigate whether Lawrence Richmond's father had any brothers who passed the Richmond family Y-DNA to a living male willing to take a Y-DNA test. This can proceed for multiple generations until the research either hits a brick wall or finds a male with the Richmond Y-DNA who is willing to take a test.

Additional research going back a generation uncovers the names of Lawrence Richmond's parents, Hiram and Susannah (Lyon) Richmond. Research also uncovers descendants of two of Lawrence Richmond's three brothers. Using the extended tree titled "Descendants of Hiram and Susannah (Lyon) Richmond," answer questions 6 and 7.

Descendants of Hiram and Susannah (Lyon) Richmond

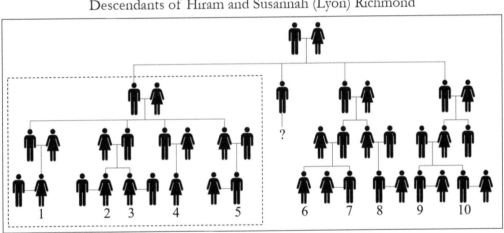

6. Hiram Richmond has ten living great-grandchildren (numbered 1 through 10). Circle everyone in the tree who should possess the Richmond family Y-DNA. Which of the great-grandchildren inherited their Y-DNA from Hiram Richmond?

Descendants of Hiram and Susannah (Lyon) Richmond

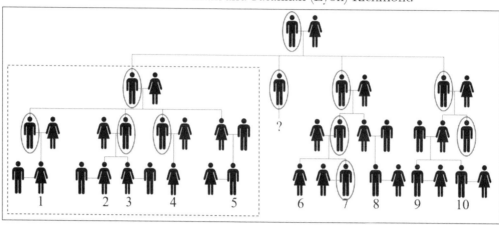

The only great-grandchild depicted in this tree with Hiram Richmond's Y-DNA is great-grandchild 7.

7. If the male great-grandchild(ren) in this chart decline to take a Y-DNA test, what other Y-DNA testing strategy could a genealogist pursue to learn about the Richmond family's Y-DNA?

> *There are several possible strategies for learning about the Richmond family Y-DNA. For example, a genealogist could try to identify the descendants, if any, of the great-grandfather's second-born son. Another strategy is to research the descendants of any brothers of the great-grandfather, and descendants of uncles of the great-grandfather, in order to identify other direct-line males willing to take a Y-DNA test.*

Use the family tree chart titled "Descendants of John and Jane [?] Albro" to answer questions 8 through 13. For some questions, it may be easiest to create a table showing the marker values for each test-taker and the path back to John Albro. To determine which markers are fast-moving, the Y-DNA quick-reference notes available on Debbie Parker Wayne's blog, *Deb's Delvings in Genealogy* (http://debsdelvings.blogspot.com/search/label/QuickRef), may be helpful.

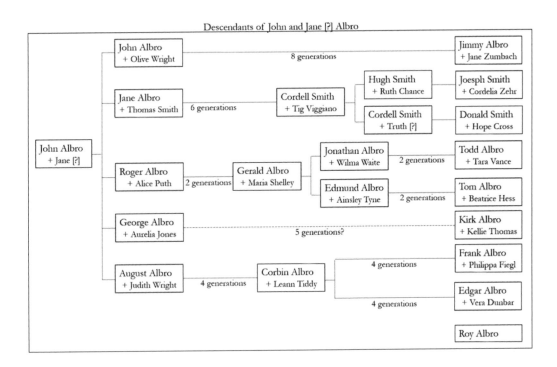

Descendants of John and Jane [?] Albro

Genealogist Roy Albro has constructed a family tree containing all known descendants of John and Jane [?] Albro of New Hampshire, numbering in the thousands. Roy believes he fits in the tree somewhere, but documentary research has not definitively placed him.

With a goal of finding additional clues, Roy tested himself and eight known descendants of John Albro using a SNP-based test from the testing company 23andMe (which provides the Y-DNA haplogroup) and a 37-marker Y-DNA test from Family Tree DNA. The combined results are provided in the following table.

	23andMe Paternal Haplogroup	DYS393	DYS390	DYS19	DYS391	DYS385	DYS426	DYS388	DYS439	DYS389i	DYS392	DYS389ii	DYS458	DYS459	DYS455	DYS454	DYS447	DYS437	DYS448	DYS449
Jimmy Albro	R1b1b2	13	24	14	10	11-14	12	12	13	13	13	29	17	9-9	10	11	25	15	19	31
Joseph Smith	R1b1b2	13	24	14	11	11-14	12	12	12	13	13	29	18	9-10	11	11	25	15	19	29
Donald Smith	R1b1b2	13	24	14	11	11-14	12	12	12	13	13	29	18	9-10	11	11	25	15	19	29
Todd Albro	R1b1b2	13	24	14	10	11-14	12	12	12	13	13	29	17	9-9	10	11	25	15	19	30
Tom Albro	R1b1b2	13	24	14	10	11-14	12	12	12	13	13	29	17	9-9	10	11	25	15	19	30
Kirk Albro	R1b1b2	13	24	14	10	11-14	12	12	13	13	13	29	17	9-9	10	11	26	15	19	30
Frank Albro	R1b1b2	13	24	14	10	11-14	12	12	12	13	13	29	17	9-9	10	11	25	15	19	30
Edgar Albro	E1b1b1a	13	23	13	10	15-16	11	12	12	13	11	31	17	9-9	12	11	25	14	20	33
Roy Albro	R1b1b2	13	24	14	10	11-14	12	12	13	13	13	29	17	9-9	10	11	26	15	19	30

	DYS464	DYS460	GATA-H4	YCAII	DYS456	DYS607	DYS576	DYS570	CDY	DYS442	DYS438	DYS531	DYS578	DYF395S1	DYS590	DYS537	DYS641	DYS472
Jimmy Albro	15-15-16-17	10	11	19-23	16	16	16	17	37-39	12	12	11	9	15-16	8	10	10	8
Joseph Smith	15-16-17-18	11	10	19-23	16	16	17	17	36-37	11	12	11	9	15-16	8	10	10	8
Donald Smith	15-16-17-18	11	10	19-23	16	16	17	17	36-37	11	12	11	9	15-16	8	10	10	8
Todd Albro	15-15-16-17	10	11	19-23	16	16	17	17	37-39	12	12	11	9	15-16	8	10	10	8
Tom Albro	15-15-16-17	10	11	19-23	16	16	17	17	37-39	12	12	11	9	15-16	8	10	10	8
Kirk Albro	15-15-16-17	10	11	19-23	16	16	17	18	37-39	12	12	11	9	15-16	8	10	10	8
Frank Albro	15-15-16-17	10	11	19-23	16	16	17	17	37-39	12	12	11	9	15-16	8	10	10	8
Edgar Albro	14-15-15-17	11	11	19-22	15	12	18	18	37-37	13	10	10	8	15-17	8	11	10	8
Roy Albro	15-15-16-17	10	11	19-23	16	16	17	18	37-39	12	12	11	9	15-16	8	10	10	8

8. Based **solely** on the 23andMe paternal haplogroup listed in the second column, could the reconstructed family tree for Jimmy Albro, Todd Albro, Tom Albro, Kirk Albro, Frank Albro, and Edgar Albro be correct?

> *Jimmy, Todd, Tom, Kirk, and Frank belong to Y-DNA haplogroup R1b1b2, while Edgar belongs to Y-DNA haplogroup E1b1b1a. Frank Albro and Edgar Albro are thought to be fourth cousins, according to Roy Albro's family tree, but they belong to very different haplogroups. Accordingly, there is at least one error in the family tree, most likely with regard to Edgar Albro.*

9. What could explain Edgar Albro's Y-DNA test results?

> *Edgar's Y-DNA belongs to a different haplogroup than all the other Albro males, although the tree indicates he is a descendant of John Albro Sr. on the patrilineal line. Since Frank matches the remainder of the Albro males, Frank's*

ancestor Corbin Albro most likely possessed the Albro Y chromosome. Thus, there was most likely a misattributed-parentage event in the line somewhere between Corbin Albro and Edgar Albro.

10. Should Joseph Smith and Donald Smith share the same Y-DNA as the Albro males? Why or why not?

No. Joseph and Donald Smith should not share Y-DNA with the Albro males, as they are descendants of John Albro's daughter.

11. Do Joseph Smith and Donald Smith share the same Y-DNA as the Albro males?

No. Although the Smiths belong to a similar haplogroup, their Y-STR haplotypes differ considerably from most of the Albro males.

12. Looking at only the results for Jimmy, Todd, Tom, Kirk, and Frank Albro, map the Y-DNA mutations to the family tree. Do the DNA results correlate logically with the family tree? Can you identify the places in the family tree where the mutations on markers DYS439, 447, 449, 576, and 570 likely occurred?

The results appear to align well with the family tree, and the mutations likely occurred in the following locations:
- *DYS439: Descendants of John and George both have 13 repeats at DYS439, while descendants of Roger and August have 12 repeats. Neither the original value nor where it may have changed is clear. DYS439 is a fast-changing marker, which may explain the results.*
- *DYS447: Only George's descendants have 26 repeats at DYS447, suggesting that the mutation arose somewhere between (and including) George and Kirk Albro.*
- *DYS449: Only Jimmy Albro has 31 repeats at DYS449, suggesting that the mutation arose somewhere between (and including) John Jr. and Jimmy Albro.*
- *DYS576: Only Jimmy Albro has 16 repeats at DYS576, suggesting that the mutation arose somewhere between (and including) John Jr. and Jimmy Albro.*
- *DYS570: Only George's descendants have 18 repeats at DYS570, suggesting that the mutation arose somewhere between (and including) George and Kirk Albro.*

13. Could Roy fit within this Albro family tree based on the results of the Y-DNA testing? Based on the results, where might he fit best?

Yes, based on the Y-DNA testing, Roy could possibly fit in the Albro family tree. Roy's results most closely match those of Kirk Albro. It is possible that Roy is a descendant of John Albro, and possibly a descendant of George Albro. It is also possible that Roy could be descended from a brother or other relative of John Albro Sr.

Walter believes his great-grandfather had Native American ancestry on the paternal line. He orders a 37-marker Y-DNA test from Family Tree DNA. Based on the results, Walter's estimated haplogroup is R1b1b2a.

14. Based on the DNA test results, is Walter's Y chromosome Native American? Could Walter's great-grandfather have had Native American ancestry on his paternal line?

> *R1b1b2a is not a Native American haplogroup, and thus Walter's Y chromosome is not Native American. Y-DNA testing rules out Native American ancestry on Walter's direct male line. It is still possible that one or more of Walter's great-grandfather's other recent ancestors could have been Native American or possessed Native American DNA.*

Luther orders a 67-marker Y-STR test from Family Tree DNA. The company predicts his haplogroup to be R. Luther orders a SNP test to further refine his placement on haplogroup R, and he receives the following results:

M207+, M173+, M343+, P297+, M269+, L23+, L51+, L151+, U106+, S263+, Z301+, L146−, Z156−

---

15. Using the 2015 version of the ISOGG Y-DNA Haplogroup R Tree (http://isogg.org/tree/ISOGG_HapgrpR15.html) and Luther's Y-SNP results, determine Luther's terminal SNP.

> *To determine Luther's terminal SNP, go to the ISOGG Y-DNA Haplogroup R Tree and plot the SNP results onto the tree. One way to do this is to construct a tree like the one below, showing the derived ("+") and ancestral SNPs, and removing branches that weren't tested. This will effectively "walk" down the Y-DNA tree to the most terminal point for the SNPs that Luther has tested. At the final branch point of Luther's tree, there are two SNPs located under the S263 SNP, meaning that some people are derived for Z156 and some people are derived for Z301. If Luther was not derived for either Z156 or Z301, his terminal SNP would be S263. However, Luther has tested both Z156 and Z301 and is derived at Z301, therefore Luther's terminal SNP is Z301. This terminal SNP is subject to change when additional SNPs under Z301 are discovered.*

R   M207+
• R1   M173+
• • R1a   L146-
• • R1b   M343+
• • • • R1b1   P297+
• • • • • R1b1a2   M269+
• • • • • • R1b1a2a   L23+
• • • • • • • R1b1a2a1   L51+
• • • • • • • • R1b1a2a1a   L151+

• • • • • • • • • R1b1a2a1a1 U106+
• • • • • • • • • • R1b1a2a1a1c S263+
• • • • • • • • • • • R1b1a2a1a1c1 Z156-
• • • • • • • • • • • • • R1b1a2a1a1c2   Z301+

Jason is adopted and searching for information about his genetic heritage. He orders a 67-marker Y-DNA test from Family Tree DNA and receives his results eight weeks later. Jason has six matches at 67 markers, including five matches at a genetic distance of three or closer.

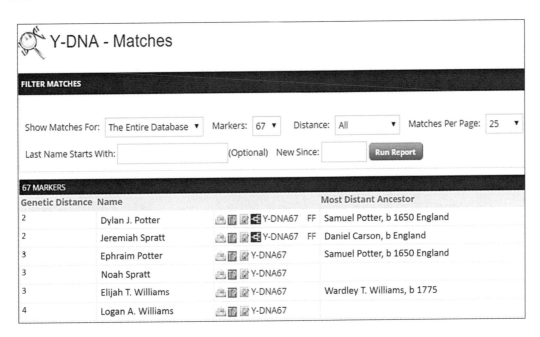

16. Can Jason make any conclusions about his biological surname based on his Y-DNA matches?

Jason cannot make any definitive conclusions about his biological surname based on these Y-DNA matches. Although he has several close Potter matches, he also has several close Spratt and Williams relatives. No surname is sufficiently definitive. Each of these potential surnames, including Potter, Spratt, and Williams, can be reviewed and considered for additional clues.

Chapter 4 Exercise Answers

Use the family tree chart in Appendix A titled "Descendants of Mary Ann (Smith) and John Ira Jones" to answer questions 1 through 3. The genealogist has confirmed that there are no common ancestors for the people named on the chart other than those shown. Each kinship link has been confirmed with strong documentary evidence.

Hint: The easiest way to answer these questions is to make a copy of the chart, then, beginning with Mary Ann Smith, mark all descendants who inherited her mtDNA. One at a time, move to women who married into the family and repeat the process, using a unique mark for each woman who contributed mtDNA to descendants.

In the following questions, a parenthesized number after an individual's name represents that person's number on the chart.

1. Which descendants shown inherited the mtDNA of Mary Ann (Smith) Jones (2)?

    The descendants who inherited Mary Ann (Smith) Jones's mtDNA are numbers 3, 4, 5, 11, 12, 21, 22, and 33.

    Mary Ann (2) passed her mtDNA to all of her children (Albert (3), Mary (4), Emma (5)). Her son Albert could not pass his mother's mtDNA to his children. His children inherited mtDNA from their mother. Mary Ann's daughter Mary Jones (4) passed her mtDNA to her son Sid (11), but Sid did not pass it to his children. Mary Ann's daughter Emma Jones (5) passed her mtDNA to her own daughter Emma (12). Emma (12) passed her mtDNA to all of her children (Mandy (21) and Max (22)). Mandy (21) passed her mtDNA to her child Mandella (33). Max did not pass his mtDNA to his children.

2. Ira Gerball (20) died while serving in Vietnam. The military has located what is believed to be his body. To provide evidence that the correct body has been identified, the military is looking for family members to take an mtDNA test. Which people on the chart share the same mtDNA as Ira?

    The people on the chart who have the same mtDNA as Ira Gerball (20) are numbers 15, 19, 31, and 43.

    Ira (20) inherited his mtDNA from his mother, Marie Small (15). Marie also passed her mtDNA to her daughter Florence Gerball (19). Florence passed her mtDNA to her own daughter Janice Johns (31). Janice passed her mtDNA to her son Ira Ryan (43). Any of these are potential mtDNA test-takers, as all should share the mtDNA of Ira Gerball (20).

3. Adoptee Angela Marks has used atDNA and documentary research to determine she may be a child of either Mandella Louise Smith (33) or Emmy Wick (34), both of whom are deceased and have no descendants shown on this chart. Both of Mandella's parents are deceased, but Emmy's parents are still living.

a. If Emmy's parents (Max Wick (22) and Emmy Martin (28)) agree to take an mtDNA test, could the results help Angela determine whether Emmy Wick (34) or Mandella Louise Smith (33) may be her mother?

Yes. The lack of a match to Max (22) or Emmy (28) could rule out one of the candidate mothers.

If Angela's mtDNA matches that of Max Wick (22), then Mandella (33) could be Angela's mother. Max and Mandella both inherited the mtDNA that was passed down from Mary Ann (Smith) Jones (2).

If Angela's mtDNA matches that of Emmy (Martin) Wick (28), then Emmy Wick (34) could be Angela's mother. Emmy (Martin) Wick passed her mtDNA to her daughter Emmy Wick (34), who would have passed it to her children.

b. What is the conclusion if Angela's mtDNA test matches both Max Wick (22) and Emmy Martin (28)? Would that double match be significant in a genealogically relevant timeframe?

The ancestry of Emmy Martin (28) is not shown on this chart. It is possible she shares a matrilineal link with Mary Ann (Smith) Jones (2). Because mtDNA mutates at a relatively low rate, a matrilineal link could be from one to many generations back in the family tree.

4. Susie Donelson and Josie McSpadden have taken full mtDNA sequence tests and are not shown on each other's list of matches. The chart below shows their mtDNA results as compared to the rCRS as well as outlines of their well-researched matrilineal lines.

	Susie Donelson mtDNA Haplogroup U5b1d1	Josie McSpadden mtDNA Haplogroup U5b1d1
HVR2		263G
CR	15607R	8542Y
HVR1	16192T	
mtDNA Lines	Tempy Gordy Sarah (Gordy) Parker Elizabeth (Parker) Richards Bonnie (Richards) Carter Mary (Carter) Vick Janice (Vick) Martin Vickie (Martin) Donelson Susie Donelson	Possibly Tempy Gordy (Speculative Link) Elizabeth (unknown) Rogers Sarah (Rogers) Bell Annie May (Bell) Kelly Martha (Kelly) Patrick Dicey (Kelly) McSpadden Josie McSpadden

a. Do the test results prove they are not related on the matrilineal line? Why or why not?

> *No, these results do not prove the two test-takers are not related. Each has one mutation and one heteroplasmy not shared with the other. The four differences would prevent either from being on the other's match list. A difference of four markers in this timeframe is rare, but not impossible, due to random mutations. These results would require a discussion of the conflict, including analysis of both the DNA and the documentary evidence supporting the conclusion of kinship.*

b. Could other kinds of DNA tests help answer this question more definitively?

> *If this speculative family link is true, Susie and Josie are fifth cousins once removed. That relationship is at the boundary where atDNA testing may or may not provide evidence to address this question (as will be discussed in the next chapter). Asking Susie and Josie to take an atDNA test would be wise, although there is a chance the test results will not provide useful information. Even if Susie and Josie do not share enough atDNA to help answer the question, one or both of them may match other test-takers who are descendants of Tempy Gordy. Analyzing all the possible evidence leads to more credible conclusions.*

5. Annabell Martin was told her fifth great-grandmother was a Cherokee who left the reservation to marry Annabell's fifth great-grandfather. Which of the following must be true for an mtDNA test to help Annabell prove this story? Mark all answers that apply.
   a. There must be a direct matrilineal line from the fifth great-grandmother to Annabell.
   b. There must be a direct matrilineal line from the fifth great-grandmother to any living descendant in the line who is willing to take a test.
   c. A full mtDNA sequence test must be used, as this provides the most conclusive evidence.
   d. A low- or medium-resolution mtDNA test should be sufficient, as the haplogroup alone is generally enough to identify Native American ancestry.
   e. At least three test-takers will be needed for conclusive proof.

Statements b and d must be true for mtDNA results to apply to this question.

Item a does not have to be true, as it is not necessary for Annabell to be the test-taker. As stated in item b, anyone who is a matrilineal-line descendant of Annabell's fifth great-grandmother is a candidate for the mtDNA test.

Item c does not have to be true, as a low- or medium-resolution mtDNA test can usually determine whether the haplogroup is one that could be Native American. A haplogroup cannot indicate a specific tribe such as Cherokee. A haplogroup indicating Native American ancestry combined with a family history in the Americas supports a conclusion of Native American ancestry that could be Cherokee or some other tribal affiliation. Documentary and historical research might help define tribal possibilities on the locations near where this family resided.

Item e does not have to be true, as mtDNA test results should be the same for any matrilineal-line descendant of Annabell's fifth great-grandmother. Because mtDNA does not recombine there is no loss of DNA in each generation. However, when one person is tested and the mtDNA is not in a Native American haplogroup, testing additional family members could be useful to be sure there was not some event (such as an unknown adoption) that caused the first tested person to inherit mtDNA from someone other than Annabell's fifth great-grandmother.

6. Two test-takers who suspect a common ancestor on the matrilineal line take medium-resolution mtDNA tests (HVR1 and HVR2). Neither appears on the match list of the other. The thoroughly researched and well-documented matrilineal lines, with known dates and places, are shown below.

Sarah's mtDNA Line	Jane's mtDNA Line
Jane (Vick) Otis, b. 1800 Rowan County, North Carolina; d. 1870 Copiah County, Mississippi	
Mary Otis, b. 1825 Rowan County, North Carolina; d. 1900 Angelina County, Texas	Elizabeth Otis, b. unknown date and place; m. 1845 Rowan County, North Carolina
Emma Ryan, b. 1860 Angelina County, Texas; d. 1940 Dallas, Texas	Martha Parrott, b. 1858 Conecuh County, Alabama; d. 1930 Conecuh County, Alabama
Joyce Johnson, b. 1890 Angelina County, Texas; d. 1960 Dallas, Texas	Dollie Richards, b. 1888 Conecuh County, Alabama; d. 1940 Conecuh County, Alabama
Sarah Richards, b. 1916 Dallas, Texas	Bonnie Jackson, b. 1920 Conecuh County, Alabama; d. 1970 Yell County, Arkansas
	Jane Smith, b. 1940 Yell County, Arkansas

a. Does the fact that these two test-takers are not on each other's match list preclude Jane (Vick) Otis from being the mother of both Mary Otis and Elizabeth Otis?

No. As explained above, there could be mtDNA mutations preventing two test-takers from appearing on a match list even when there is a proven matrilineal-line connection.

b. Would it be advantageous for Sarah and Jane to upgrade to a full mtDNA sequence test?

Upgrading to a full mtDNA sequence test could provide more useful mtDNA data to apply to this problem.

c. What other things might be considered based on the lineages shown?

*The fact that Jane (Vick) Otis, Mary Otis, and Elizabeth Otis share a surname;
that the three women were all in Rowan County, North Carolina, at about the
same time; and that Jane is of an age to be the mother of Mary and Elizabeth,
does not prove the mother-daughter relationships—even with an exact match on
a full mtDNA sequence. If research in Rowan County shows there were no other
Otis families in the area, that fact, combined with the mtDNA test results,
provides a strong reason to focus on this Otis family in the search for other
evidence linking Jane as the mother of Mary and Elizabeth.*

7. Sarah and Jane upgrade to full mtDNA sequence tests and receive the results below.
Neither appears on the match list of the other.

Sarah's full mtDNA sequence test results	
Haplogroup	U5b1d1c
HVR1 differences from rCRS	16192T, 16218T, 16270T, 16320T
HVR2 differences from rCRS	73G, 150T, 263G, 315.1C, 523.1C. 523.2A
Coding Region differences from rCRS	750G, 1438G, 2706G, 3197C, 4769G, 5437T, 5656G, 7028T, 7768G, 7912A, 8860G, **9138Y**, 9477A, 11476G, 11719A, 12308G, 12372A, 13617C, 14182C, 14766T, 14326G, 15631G, 15721C

Jane's full mtDNA sequence test results	
Haplogroup	U5b1d1c
HVR1 differences from rCRS	16192T, **16193R**, 16218T, 16270T, 16320T
HVR2 differences from rCRS	73G, 150T, 263G, 315.1C, 523.1C. 523.2A
Coding Region differences from rCRS	750G, 1438G, 2706G, 3197C, 4769G, 5437T, 5656G, **6260R**, 7028T, 7768G, 7912A, 8860G, 9477A, 11476G, 11719A, 12308G, 12372A, 13617C, 14182C, 14766T, 14326G, **15326G**, 15631G, 15721C

a. Does the fact that these two test-takers are not on each other's match list
preclude Jane (Vick) Otis from being the mother of both Mary Otis and Elizabeth
Otis? Do these results prove Jane is the mother of Mary and Elizabeth?

*These test results neither preclude Jane (Vick) Otis from being the mother of both
Mary Otis and Elizabeth Otis, nor prove Jane is the mother.*

b. Do these results explain why neither appears on the match list of the other?

*The test-takers do not appear on one another's match list because of the four-step
difference between the testers in the full mtDNA sequence and the one-step*

difference in the HVR1/HVR2 test. These differences fall outside of the thresholds for inclusion on a match list.

c. What do the Ys and Rs in the list of mtDNA differences (shown in bold above) from the reference sequence mean?

The Ys and Rs indicate heteroplasmies found in the mtDNA test results of both test-takers. Jane has differences at location 16193 and 6260. Both of these are heteroplasmies; the R indicates both locations carry some mitochondria with an A and some mitochondria with a G. Sarah has a heteroplasmy at location 9138; the Y indicates there are some mitochondria with a T and some mitochondria with a C at this location.

The proof discussion of the mtDNA evidence could argue for a close relationship between Jane and Sarah if both of their heteroplasmic locations contain the same value (GCAT). For example, Jane's heteroplasmy at location 6260 indicates some mitochondria carry an A and some a G. If Sarah has either an A or a G at location 6260, her mtDNA matches some of Jane's mtDNA at this location.

Chapter 5 Exercise Answers

1. Sisters Karen (Johnson) Whitmore and Carrie (Johnson) Philips have received their results from an AncestryDNA test. The results indicate they are full sisters, sharing approximately 2,430 cM. When reviewing their genetic matches, Carrie notices that Karen shares a close match with an Ancestry user named "ThomasJohnson" who is predicted to be their third cousin with a possible range of third to fourth cousin. The user's tree reveals that "ThomasJohnson" is indeed their third cousin once removed. But when Carrie reviews her own results, she doesn't see "ThomasJohnson" as a match. Should Carrie expect "ThomasJohnson" to be in her match list? What could explain the absence?

   Since Karen and Carrie are full siblings, the reason "ThomasJohnson" is not appearing in Carrie's results is that she has randomly failed to inherit a sufficient amount of DNA in common with "ThomasJohnson." As shown in table 4 of this chapter, a portion of which is reproduced below, third cousins have between a 90 and 98 percent chance of sharing a detectable amount of DNA, while fourth cousins have between a 45 and 71 percent chance of sharing a detectable amount of DNA. A third cousin once removed should fall somewhere between these probability ranges.

Relationship	23andMe (%)	AncestryDNA (%)	Family Tree DNA (%)
Third cousin	~90	98	>90
Fourth cousin	~45	71	>50

   Accordingly, it is not surprising that Karen and "ThomasJohnson" share a detectable amount of DNA and are predicted to be third to fourth cousins, and neither is it surprising that Carrie and "ThomasJohnson" fail to share a detectable amount of DNA.

2. Fred is testing numerous relatives in an attempt to map his chromosomes and characterize his genetic family tree. He does not share any detectable DNA with Victoria, a seventh cousin through shared fifth great-grandparents John and Helen Quincy. Can Fred conclude that John and Helen Quincy are not in his genetic family tree?

   Not based on this result alone. To share any DNA with Victoria, they both must have obtained the same segment of DNA from John or Helen Quincy, which at the seventh cousin level is a very remote possibility. One or both of Fred and Victoria may have John or Helen Quincy, or both, in their genetic family trees, but they do not have the same segment or segments of DNA from those ancestors. It is also possible that neither Fred nor Victoria has John or Helen Quincy in their genetic family trees, but this cannot be determined from this test alone.

3. Roy and Mike share a single 6.43 cM DNA segment on chromosome 3. Of 23andMe, AncestryDNA, and Family Tree DNA, which company or companies will identify Roy

and Mike as genetic relatives? Which company or companies will not identify Roy and Mike as genetic relatives?

Roy and Mike will not be identified as genetic cousins at 23andMe, where the threshold is 7 cM and at least 700 SNPs for the first segment of atDNA. They will also not be identified as genetic cousins at Family Tree DNA, where the threshold is either a minimum 9 cM segment, or a minimum 7.69 cM segment with a total shared 20 cM. Roy and Mike may be identified as genetic matches at AncestryDNA, where the threshold is 5 cM if the segment survives the algorithm that identifies pile-up regions.

4. One cM is equivalent to a 1 percent (one in one hundred) probability of a recombination event occurring somewhere within that DNA segment within a single generation. Is it possible to share a DNA segment of 100 cM or greater with a relative (other than a parent passing down entire chromosomes to a child)?

Yes, it is possible to share a DNA segment of 100 cM or more with a relative other than a parent. The cM is only a probability of a recombination event occurring. Due to the randomness of recombination it is possible for a segment equal to or larger than 100 cM to be transmitted in its entirety for multiple generations. Other than parent/child relationships, segments equal to or greater than 100 cM will be most commonly observed in grandparent/grandchild and aunt/uncle/niece/nephew relationships. By the very next generation—great-grandparent/great-grandchild and first cousins—the probability of sharing a segment of 100 cM or larger is significantly reduced, but it can still be observed.

5. Viktor has tested his parents but not himself. His grandparents are living but he has not yet tested them because, he reasons, all the DNA he inherited from them was tested when Viktor tested his parents. He has an aunt, a first cousin, two second cousins, and a third cousin, all of whom are willing to test. Whom should Viktor test first?

Viktor should first ask his grandparents to take a DNA test. Although Viktor is correct that by testing his parents he tested all of the DNA that Viktor inherited from his grandparents, this testing does not capture the 50 percent of DNA from each grandparent that the parents did not inherit. Additionally, a cardinal rule of genetic genealogy is to test the oldest generation first. This ensures that they are available to test.

Referring to table 5 in this chapter, after the grandparents are tested Viktor should ask the second cousins followed by the third cousin. The aunt and first cousin should be last, if at all; Viktor effectively tested any DNA he shares with them when he tested the grandparents he shares with them.

6. Sally has tested three of her grandparents. Her paternal grandfather is deceased and thus cannot be tested. The results show she shares the following amounts of DNA with her three tested grandparents:

	Paternal Grandmother	Maternal Grandfather	Maternal Grandmother
Amount of DNA Shared (%)	28.6	23.5	26.5

Based on this information, what percentage of DNA did Sally inherit from her untested paternal grandfather?

Sally knows she had to inherit 50 percent of her DNA from each parent, and 100 percent of her DNA from her four grandparents. By adding together the DNA she inherited from her three tested grandparents (28.6+23.5+26.5=78.6) and subtracting that total from 100 percent, she calculates that she must have inherited approximately 21.4 percent of her DNA from her paternal grandfather.

The following is a chromosome-browser comparison of a paternal grandmother and her granddaughter, showing where they share DNA on chromosome 1. During meiosis, the father took the copies of chromosome 1 that he received from his father and from his mother and recombined—or didn't recombine—the chromosomes. The black box indicates the chromosome, and the shaded areas indicate the segments shared by the paternal grandmother and her granddaughter. Use the diagram to answer questions 7 and 8.

7. Place an arrow (or arrows) showing where the recombination events must have occurred. How many recombination events occurred on chromosome 1?

   There must have been three different recombination events on chromosome 1, as shown below:

   If there had been only a single recombination event at one of the arrows, the chromosome browser would resemble one of the following:

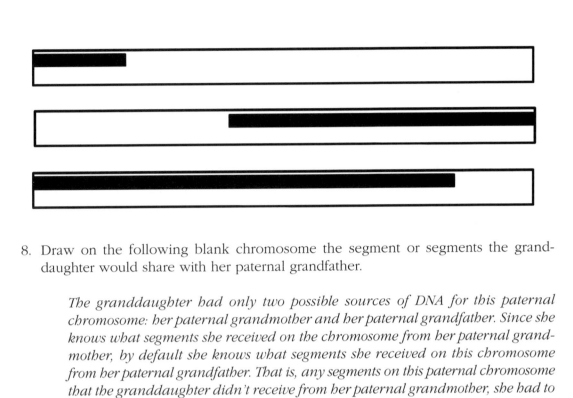

8. Draw on the following blank chromosome the segment or segments the granddaughter would share with her paternal grandfather.

   The granddaughter had only two possible sources of DNA for this paternal chromosome: her paternal grandmother and her paternal grandfather. Since she knows what segments she received on the chromosome from her paternal grandmother, by default she knows what segments she received on this chromosome from her paternal grandfather. That is, any segments on this paternal chromosome that the granddaughter didn't receive from her paternal grandmother, she had to receive from her paternal grandfather. The segments from the paternal grandfather on chromosome 1 will look like this:

   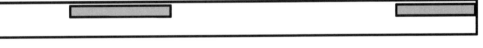

   And together with the segments from the paternal grandmother, the chromosome browser would look like this:

9. Laura has tested herself and her grandmother Brenda. On chromosome 4, they share the following DNA segments:

   Laura has also tested her son Michael and would like to compare Michael's DNA to that of his great-grandmother Brenda. Which of the following chromosome-browser views might Laura expect to see when comparing Michael and Brenda?

Technically all options are possible, although a through c are the most likely. For options a and b to be true, one or more recombination events resulted in some but not all of Brenda's DNA being passed down to Michael. For option c to be true, no DNA on this chromosome was passed down to Michael.

Option d requires that Michael's father shared a segment of DNA with Brenda. The smaller segment of DNA on the chromosome in option d could not have come from Laura, since it wasn't in her comparison to her grandmother; it must have come from Michael's father instead. The likelihood of seeing this is much, much lower than answers a, b, and c.

Use the family tree chart titled "Relatives of Violet Redden" to answer questions 10 through 15.

Relatives of Violet Redden

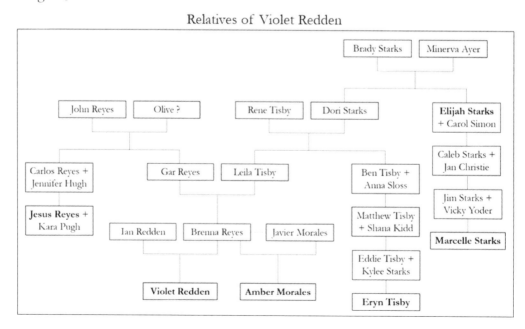

10. Violet Redden, the family genealogist, has tested herself as well as five of her family members (**bold** in the family tree). Complete the table below, determining (a) relationship to Violet, and (b) expected amount of shared DNA (in percentage and in cM).

Relative	Expected Relationship to Violate Redden	Expected % of DNA in Common	Expected cM of DNA in Common
Jesus Reyes	*First cousin once removed*	6.25	425
Amber Morales	*Half sister*	25	1700
Eryn Tisby	*Second cousin once removed*	1.563	106.25
Elijah Starks	*Great granduncle*	6.25	425
Marcelle Starks	*Third cousin*	0.781	53.13

11. Violet receives Eryn Tisby's results and discovers that Eryn shares 205 cM of DNA with Marcelle Starks. How does that result align with the family tree? If the result is unexpected, what piece of information from the tree might explain the result?

> *According to the tree, Eryn and Marcelle are third cousins once removed and should share about 0.391 percent (26.56 cM) of their DNA. The result, however, suggests they are much more recently related along another line. Reviewing the available information, we see that Eryn's mother is Kylee Starks, and that Eryn and Marcelle may be related on the Starks line multiple times—including a more recent relationship than Brady and Minerva (Ayer) Starks. Additional research may identify the currently unknown shared ancestry between Eryn and Marcelle.*

Violet downloads her raw data and the raw data of Eryn Tisby, Elijah Starks, and Marcelle Starks. She uploads that raw data to GEDmatch to obtain information about the segments of DNA she shares with each of these relatives. The following table is a sample of some of the segments that Violet shares with Eryn, Elijah, and Marcelle. Use this table to answer questions 12 through 14.

Relative	Chromosome	Start Location	End Location	cM
Eryn Tisby	1	61687081	109171900	37.05
	5	14343689	26724511	12.58
	12	78977472	93650661	13.96
Elijah Starks	2	39940529	61792229	21.54
	18	11751127	36127946	18.9
	20	39812713	64231310	22.82
Marcelle Starks	8	11176816	16565963	10.56
	18	11751127	36127946	18.9

12. Determine the most distant ancestor or ancestors in the tree to whom the DNA segment that Violet shares with Elijah Starks on chromosome 18 can be tentatively mapped.

   The segment can be tentatively mapped to Brady and Minerva (Ayer) Starks, as they are the most recent common ancestors shared by Violet and Elijah. However, the possibility exists that Violet and Elijah share other ancestors, either known or unknown.

13. Determine the ancestor or ancestors in the tree to whom the DNA segments that Violet shares with Eryn Tisby on chromosomes 1, 5, and 12 can be tentatively mapped.

   Currently, the segments of DNA shared by Violet and Eryn cannot be reliably mapped to any ancestors in the tree. The unusually high amount of shared DNA between Eryn Tisby and Marcelle, for example, suggests multiple lines of sharing that could affect the mapping.

14. Based on the information in the tree and the table, describe what is unusual about the DNA that Marcelle Starks shares with Violet.

   Marcelle shares a segment of DNA on chromosome 8 with Violet, but Marcelle's great-grandfather Elijah fails to share that segment. Marcelle should not share any DNA with Violet that Elijah doesn't share with Violet, and thus Marcelle must have inherited that segment from another line that she and Violet have in common.

15. A chromosome browser reveals the following pattern on chromosome 5, with three genetic matches sharing a long segment of DNA (35 cM, 50 cM, and 75 cM) with the test-taker:

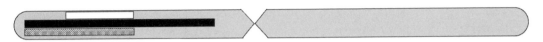

Based on this view, what do we know about the genetic relationship of each of the three individuals to one another?

Essentially, we know very little about the genetic relationships of the three individuals. A chromosome browser only shows where a test-taker shares DNA with genetic matches, it does not show where two genetic matches share DNA with one another. Thus, to learn about the genetic relationships we must either use the ICW tool to deduce this information (with the limitations that accompany ICW), or contact the matches to inquire about sharing with the other individuals depicted. Since the test-taker can only match these three individuals on one or two chromosomes, and because these segments are too large to be false positives, we do know that at least two—and possibly all three—of the individuals must share the overlapping region.

The following table was generated using segment data and Family Tree DNA's Matrix tool. The Matrix tool reveals whether two people share one or more DNA segments, but the tool does not reveal exactly what segment or segments are shared. In the table, shared DNA is indicated by an "x." Use this table to answer questions 16 and 17.

Chr	Start	End	cM	Name	Brenda	Ellen	Leonard	Susan	Johnny	Aaron	Georgia	Shana	Donna
1	207845978	247093448	57.02	Brenda			X					X	
1	231686686	236689066	11.11	Ellen				X	X		X		X
1	231875734	238703639	14.13	Leonard	X							X	
1	232679618	236689066	8.73	Susan		X			X		X		X
1	232679618	236689066	8.73	Johnny		X		X			X		X
1	233845007	236689066	6.32	Aaron									
1	234808789	234108935	18.43	Georgia		X		X	X				X
1	235328384	234108935	17.09	Shana	X		X						
1	235328384	243660729	18.66	Donna		X		X	X				

16. Place the nine individuals listed in the table into potential triangulation groups based on the segment data and the Matrix tool results.

    Brenda, Leonard, and Shana are in one potential triangulation group. Ellen, Susan, Johnny, Georgia, and Donna are in another potential triangulation group. Aaron does not fit within either group, and therefore must be a false positive. This highlights one of the dangers of triangulation, namely that small segments of DNA can be false-positive matches.

17. What is the limitation of using this approach for triangulation? What additional piece of information would you seek to verify that these potential groups are true triangulation groups?

Although the Matrix or ICW tool establishes that pairings within a potential triangulation group share some DNA, there is no guarantee that all members of the potential triangulation group share the segment of interest. For example, Brenda and Leonard share some DNA, but the Matrix or ICW tool does not reveal if that is the overlapping segment on chromosome 1 depicted in the table. It might be that segment, or it might be a different segment. To seek verification of these potential triangulation groups as true triangulation groups, it is necessary to determine whether the members of a potential group actually share the segment of interest.

18. Using the table below, calculate the completeness of your genealogical family tree back at least seven generations (to sixth cousin relationships), where completeness is the percentage of ancestors for whom you have a name or some identifying information. Consider the reliability or accuracy of that information, especially in the older generations where most distant-cousin relationships are being compared. How might this impact the search for shared ancestry with identified genetic matches? (The "Total # of Possible Ancestors" column may change if there have been recent cousin marriages.)

Generation	Matches	By Generation			
		Total # of Possible Ancestors	Total # of *Known* Ancestors	Total % of *Known* Ancestors	Total % of *Unknown* Ancestors
Grandparent	1st cousins	4			
G-Grandparent	2nd cousins	8			
2G-Grandparent	3rd cousins	16			
3G-Grandparent	4th cousins	32			
4G-Grandparent	5th cousins	64			
5G-Grandparent	6th cousins	128			

The following is an example of a table of tree completeness:

Generation	Matches	By Generation			
		Total # of Possible Ancestors	Total # of *Known* Ancestors	Total % of *Known* Ancestors	Total % of *Unknown* Ancestors
Grandparent	1st cousins	4	4	100	0
G-Grandparent	2nd cousins	8	8	100	0
2G-Grandparent	3rd cousins	16	14	87.5	12.5
3G-Grandparent	4th cousins	32	28	87.5	12.5
4G-Grandparent	5th cousins	64	50	78.1	21.9
5G-Grandparent	6th cousins	128	77	60.2	39.8

This table (which does not account for reliability or accuracy) demonstrates the challenges of correctly identifying a common ancestor more distant than a few generations. When comparing to relatives in the fifth- or sixth-cousin range, for example, 20 to 40 percent of the potential common ancestors are not being considered. The problem is further complicated by the completeness or incompleteness of a genetic match's family tree.

19. Angeline would like to identify the unknown parents of her fourth great-grandfather John Williams, who was born in Massachusetts in the 1750s, but she has nearly exhausted the documentary research and has found only a few clues. She has identified thirty-five living descendants of various sons of John Williams, although none are on the Y-DNA line; each of his sons' lines appear to have daughtered out in the first few generations. Angeline wonders if atDNA testing may reveal the identity of John Williams's parents. Can Angeline use atDNA for this research project? If not, why not? If so, how many descendants should she test?

Angeline could potentially use atDNA for this project. It is very likely that Angeline and most of the other identified descendants carry one or more segments of John Williams's DNA, and thus DNA from one or both of his parents. The challenge will be identifying those DNA segments. Although Angeline and most of the other identified descendants will carry segments, the vast majority will be distinct and non-overlapping. A few of the segments may be shared by two or more descendants, but those descendants must be very careful to consider possible sharing on other lines. It will be worthwhile to pursue multiple avenues of DNA research, including looking for surname patterns and locations in and around the place in Massachusetts where John Williams was born as well as target-testing descendants of John's potential parents (which has a low probability of success and is prone to many issues).

Angeline will likely have to test many of John William's descendants to arrive at a reliable conclusion. She can start with as few as two, such as herself and another descendant (preferably someone with no common ancestor other than John Williams), but ultimately she will have to add many other cousins, perhaps even dozens, to this project.

20. David Welch believes his great-great-grandfather George Smith was part Native American. There is no documentary evidence to support the belief, so David turned to atDNA testing in hopes of detecting Native American ethnicity. The testing company reported that he has no detectable amount of Native American ancestry. How does this result impact David's hypothesis?

The lack of a reported ethnicity in an ethnicity prediction is only sometimes useful evidence. If the ethnicity was very recent and was expected to be found at a significant level, then not finding it in an ethnicity report may be informative. However, if the ethnicity was back a number of generations or the ethnicity was not possessed in a significant amount by the ancestor of interest, then not finding the ethnicity in the estimate will not be informative.

Here, David's great-great-grandfather was likely not 100 percent Native American, if he was Native American at all. Any Native American DNA that David could have inherited was already reduced. Since David inherited only about 6.25 percent of his great-great-grandfather's DNA, the likelihood that the 6.25 percent contained any of the Native American DNA is very small.

Chapter 6 Exercise Answers

Use the family tree chart in Appendix A titled "Descendants of John Ira Jones and Mary Ann (Smith) Jones" to answer questions 1 through 7. The genealogist has confirmed that there are no common ancestors for the people named on the chart other than those shown. Each kinship link has been confirmed with strong documentary evidence.

Hint: The easiest way to answer these questions is to make a copy of the chart, then, beginning with Mary Ann Smith, uniquely mark all descendants who may have inherited X-DNA from her. Next move to John Ira Jones and uniquely mark all descendants who might have inherited X-DNA from him. Continue moving to people who married into the family and repeat the process for each, using a different mark for each person.

Each question considers only the ancestors shown on the chart. In real situations lines not shown on the chart must also be considered, but space does not allow inclusion of in-depth trees for every person named in this exercise. In a real scenario, the same analysis used to answer the questions about the ancestors on the chart would be applied to the complete family trees of all persons involved in the research problem.

In the following questions, a parenthesized number after an individual's name represents that person's number on the chart.

1. Which ancestors shown may have contributed to the X-DNA of Ira Gerball (20)?

   On this chart, only Marie Small (15) contributed to the X-DNA of Ira Gerball (20). Ira inherited only one X chromosome, which came from his mother, Marie. None of her ancestors are shown on this chart. Ira did not inherit an X chromosome from his father.

2. Which ancestors shown may have contributed to the X-DNA of Mandella Louise Smith (33)? Would Mandella have inherited X-DNA from all of these possible ancestors?

   Ancestors on this chart who may have contributed to the X-DNA of Mandella Louise Smith (33) are numbers 1, 2, 5, 8, 12, 16, 21, and 27. Due to random recombination some of these ancestors may not have contributed detectable amounts of X-DNA to Mandella.

   On this chart, the X-DNA of Mandella Louise Smith (33) was inherited from her mother and father, Mandy Wick (21) and Dan Smith (27). Dan's X-DNA came from his mother, who is not shown on this chart. Mandy's X-DNA came from her mother and father, Emma Crocker (12) and Tom Wick (16). Tom's X-DNA came from his mother, who is not shown on this chart. Emma Crocker's X-DNA came from her mother and father, Emma Jones (5) and Henry Crocker (8). Henry's X-DNA came from his mother, who is not shown on this chart. Emma Jones's X-DNA came from her mother and father, Mary Ann Smith (2) and John Ira Jones (1).

3. Does Louis Gerball (32) share an X-DNA inheritance line with Mandella Louise Smith (33) through the ancestors shown on this chart?

   No. Mandella's X-DNA inheritance line is described above. The only person on this chart from whom Louis Gerball inherited X-DNA is his mother, Ann Ricks (26). Ann is not in Mandella's X-DNA inheritance line.

4. Does Ira Ryan (43) share an X-DNA inheritance line with Mandella Louise Smith (33) through the ancestors shown on this chart?

   Yes. Mandella's X-DNA inheritance line is described above. The X-DNA of Ira (43) was inherited from his mother, Janice Johns (31). Janice inherited X-DNA from her mother and father, Florence Gerball (19) and Jack Johns (25). Jack's X-DNA came from his mother, who is not shown on this chart. Florence inherited X-DNA from her mother and father, Marie Small (15) and Sid Gerball (11). Marie's ancestors are not shown on this chart. Sid inherited X-DNA from his mother, Mary Jones (4). Mary Jones inherited X-DNA from her mother and father, Mary Ann Smith (2) and John Ira Jones (1).

   The only X-DNA inheritance line shown on this chart that is shared by Ira (43) and Mandella (33) is from John Ira Jones (1) and Mary Ann Smith (2).

5. Does Viola Scott (17) share an X-DNA inheritance line with Ellis Jones (10) through the ancestors shown on this chart?

   Yes, through Martha Jackson (6).

   The X-DNA of Ellis Jones (10) was inherited from his mother, Martha Jackson (6). Martha's ancestors are not shown on this chart. Viola Scott (17) inherited X-DNA from her mother and father, Viola Jones (9) and John Scott (13). John's ancestors are not shown on this chart. The X-DNA of Viola Jones (9) was inherited from her mother and father, Martha Jackson (6) and Albert Jones (3). Martha Jackson (6) is the only shared ancestor in the X-DNA lines shown on this chart for Viola (17) and Ellis (10).

6. Given the following X-DNA match results for Mandella Louise Smith (33), is the shared-segment size large enough for a genealogist to focus research for a common ancestor on those who could have contributed to the X-DNA of the test-takers? Start and stop locations have been rounded.

Name	Chr	Start	Stop	cM	SNPs
Emmy Wick (34)	X	92.7	122.4	32.00	3,450
Violet Sweets (29)	X	103.3	112.9	7.53	850
Janice Johns (31)	X	104.6	112.9	7.15	750

Yes, the segment shared with Emmy Wick is well over 10cM in size. Although the segments shared with Violet Sweets and Janice Johns are smaller, they are over 7cM in size and are overlapped by the larger segment shared with Emmy Wick. It is possible that all four cousins inherited the X-DNA from the same ancestor, assuming they share an X-DNA inheritance path.

7. Which ancestors shown on the chart are potential common ancestors who could have contributed the matching X-chromosome segment?

   The most recent common ancestor in the X-DNA inheritance path of Mandella (33) and Emmy Wick (34) is Emma Crocker (12). Mandella and Emmy share an X-DNA segment of a significant size, which may have been passed down from John Ira Jones (1) or Mary Ann Smith (2) through Emma Jones (5) to Emma Crocker (12) and ultimately to Mandella (33) and Emmy (34). Mandella and Emmy also share Henry Crocker (8) in the X-DNA inheritance path. Henry passed on intact the X chromosome inherited from his mother. The X-DNA shared by Mandella and Emmy could not have come from Tom Wick (16), as Tom did not pass an X chromosome to his son Max (22). The only shared ancestor of Violet Sweets (29) and Janice Johns (31) in the X-DNA inheritance path is Mary Ann Smith (2). Mary Ann Smith (2) is the only person in the X-DNA inheritance path shared by all four of the test-takers.

   As long as the family trees of all of these test-takers are well researched and complete on all of the X-DNA inheritance lines and there are no other common ancestors on those lines, it is probable that the shared X-DNA was inherited from Mary Ann (2). If any of the test-takers have an incomplete X-DNA inheritance line within the last five to ten generations (or so), it is possible there is a second common ancestor from whom this shared X-DNA segment may have come. If other cousins in Mary's X-DNA inheritance line have robust and full trees, testing those other cousins could provide evidence to determine if this shared segment came from another yet-unknown ancestor.

8. An X-DNA segment of a significant size is shared by Debbie, Debbie's full brother, and test-taker Allen Jackson. On which portions of the trees of these test-takers should the search for a common ancestor focus?

   The focus should be on the maternal lines of the trees belonging to Debbie and Allen. Debbie's brother inherited X-DNA only from their mother. He did not inherit any X-DNA from their father, so the paternal portion of his tree can be eliminated. Since the brother shares X-DNA with Debbie, it must have come to her from her mother, so the paternal portion of her tree can be eliminated. Allen inherited X-DNA only from his mother. He did not inherit any X-DNA from his father, so the paternal portion of his tree can be eliminated. This reduces the number of lines to be searched for a common ancestor. By completing an X-DNA inheritance chart for Allen and Debbie's brother, the number of lines can be reduced further to only those that may have contributed to the X-DNA of the two men.

9. An X-DNA segment of a significant size is shared by Debbie, Debbie's half-brother (son of Debbie's mother), and test-taker Allen Jackson. On which portions of the trees of these test-takers should the search for a common ancestor focus?

   The answer is the same as for question 7.

10. An X-DNA segment of a significant size is shared by Debbie, Debbie's half-brother (son of Debbie's father), and test-taker Allen Jackson. On which portions of the trees of these test-takers should the search for a common ancestor focus?

    The focus should be on all lines of the tree belonging to Debbie, on the maternal lines of Debbie's half-brother's tree, and on the maternal lines of Allen's tree. Debbie's brother inherited X-DNA only from his mother. He did not inherit any X-DNA from his father, so the paternal portion of his tree can be eliminated. Since he shares X-DNA with Debbie, the two likely share an X-DNA ancestor through a common ancestor in Debbie's tree and the brother's maternal tree, even though their common parent is their father. Allen inherited X-DNA only from his mother. He did not inherit any X-DNA from his father, so the paternal portion of his tree can be eliminated. This reduces the number of lines to be searched for a common ancestor. By completing an X-DNA inheritance chart for Allen, Debbie, and Debbie's brother, the number of lines can be reduced further to only those that may have contributed to the X-DNA of all three.

Chapter 7 Exercise Answers

Use the family tree chart in Appendix A titled "Descendants of Henry Smith" to answer questions 1 through 7. The genealogist has confirmed that there are no common ancestors for the people named on the chart other than those shown. Each kinship link has been confirmed with strong documentary evidence except where indicated in the exercises.

Shaded marker names in the Y-STR tables represent fast-moving markers. Markers not displayed in the table are assumed to match exactly on all men tested.

> In the following questions, a parenthesized number before or after an individual's name represents that person's number on the chart.

1. Family legend indicates Henry Smith (1) married a Native American Choctaw woman. There are five generations between that woman and the descendants at the end of each line. While an atDNA test would likely indicate some Native American DNA in at least some of the descendants, there is a possibility the Native American atDNA was lost to random recombination and inheritance patterns. An mtDNA test could provide definitive proof if there is a living descendant who inherited the woman's mtDNA. Assuming only the end-of-line descendants (the last person or persons in each column) are still living, is there anyone living who inherited the mtDNA of the unknown spouse (2) of Henry Smith (1)?

   The mtDNA of woman 2 was inherited by only one living person on this chart— Tommy Curtis (41).

2. Assume a living person is found and agrees to test, and that the test results indicate the mtDNA haplogroup is U5b1d1. Does this confirm or refute the family legend that Henry's unknown spouse (2) was Choctaw?

   The only mtDNA haplogroups known to be of Native American origin are in the branches A, B, C, D, and X. U5 and its sub-clades are not of Native American origin. If the tested person is in the matrilineal line from Henry's wife she could not have been of Choctaw origins on her direct matrilineal line. She may have been Choctaw on her other lines, however.

3. Assuming only the end-of-line descendants are still living, is there anyone living who inherited the Y-DNA of Henry Smith (1)?

   Living men who inherited Henry's Y-DNA and are potential Y-DNA testers include Ira Smith (43), Louis Smith Jr. (44), Robert Smith (33), Bobby Jack Smith (45), and Alfred Smith Jr. (46).

4. George Smith (4) is believed to be the son of Henry Smith (1). The documentary evidence is weak and there are two George Smiths of the same general age in the same location at the same time. The goal is to prove that George Smith (4) is the son

of Henry Smith (1). Two men— Ira Smith (43) and Robert Smith (33)—take a 37-marker Y-DNA STR test. Partial results are shown in the table below. Robert (33) also took a SNP test. The two men have different haplogroups displayed. Does this mean there is no way they can be related? It may be helpful to reference the 2015 version of the ISOGG Y-DNA Haplogroup R Tree (http://isogg.org/tree/ISOGG_HapgrpR15.htm) to answer this question.

Test-taker	Haplo-group	DYS 393	DYS 390	...	DYS 449	DYS 464	...	DYS 607	...	CDY	...
Ira (43)	R-M512	13	25		31	12-15-15-16		14		35-39	
Robert (33)	R-M198	13	25		31	12-15-16-16		14		35-38	

No. In this case, Robert (33) took a Y-SNP test that confirmed his terminal SNP as M198, but the predicted terminal SNP for Ira (43), M512, is based only on the Y-STR test. When we look at the R section of the Y-DNA haplotree we see that both SNP M512 and SNP M198 are on the same branch—the branch also known as R1a1a. The men are in the same haplogroup, even though the value displayed in the table is different. Being in the same haplogroup simply indicates the men share a common ancestor thousands of years back in time and they might share a more recent common ancestor.

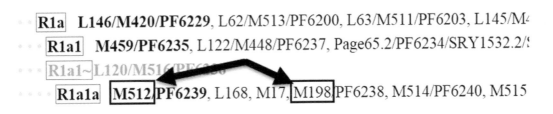

Analysis of the STR-marker values may provide more evidence to answer the questions. Correlate the STR-marker values from the table above with the "Descendants of Henry Smith" tree.

5. Ira and Robert do not match on markers DYS464 and CDY. As explained in the Y-DNA chapter, two test-takers are related when they differ on two to three markers at 37 markers tested. Does this prove George Smith (4) is the son of Henry Smith (1)?

Not conclusively. Ira (43) and Robert (33) are related and they share a common ancestor in the patrilineal line, but the Y-DNA test does not necessarily indicate that George (4) is the son of Henry (1), even when the documentary research from Ira (43) back to George (4) is conclusive. We might want to test more descendants of Henry Smith (1). We might also want to test descendants of the other George Smith who lived in this same area for comparison purposes.

6. Research continues by testing more descendants of Henry Smith (1), with the results shown in the table below. Describe the significance of the marker differences as related to the goal of determining whether Henry Smith (1) could be the father of George Smith (4). Note: It is not indicated in this table, but all other men in the Smith Surname Project who carry similar haplotypes to these men have marker DYS607=15. Use this data to answer this question's sub-parts.

Test-taker	Haplo-group	DYS 393	DYS 390	...	DYS 449	DYS 464	...	DYS 607	...	CDY	...
Ira (43)	R-M512	13	25	...	31	12-15-15-16	...	14	...	35-39	...
Robert (33)	R-M198	13	25	...	31	12-15-16-16	...	14	...	35-38	...
Louis Jr. (44)	R-M512	13	25	...	30	12-15-16-16	...	14	...	35-39	...
Bobby (45)	R-M512	13	25	...	31	12-15-16-16	...	14	...	35-39	...
Alfred Jr. (46)	R-M512	13	25	...	31	12-15-16-16	...	14	...	35-39	...

All of these men have the same values for markers DYS393, DYS390, and DYS607.

All of these men have marker DYS607=14, but other men in the surname project have this marker value as 15. Those other men may be related, but the common ancestor is further back than Henry (1).

a. All tested descendants of Henry (1) share DYS607=14. What does this tell us about Henry (1)?

This marker value probably was passed from Henry (1) to his sons, who then passed it to their sons and so on, down to living descendants.

b. All tested descendants of Henry (1) share DYS607=14. What does this tell us about Ira (43)?

He may also be a descendant of Henry (1), as Ira (43) also has DYS607=14.

c. All descendants of Henry Jr. (5) have marker DYS464=12-15-16-16, while Ira (43) has DYS464=12-15-15-16. What does this tell us about a potential link between Henry (1) and George (4)?

The marker values are consistent with George (4) being a son of Henry (1) if there was a mutation passed from Henry (1) to Henry Jr. (5) or George (4), or from Henry Jr. (5) to his son Alex (12).

d. Marker DYS449=30 for Louis Jr. (44), but DYS449=31 for the other tested men. What does this tell us about where this change may have occurred?

The change could have occurred in Ira (20), Louis (32), or Louis Jr. (44). It cannot be narrowed any further by testing the men shown in the family chart.

e. Marker CDY=35-38 for Robert (33), but CDY=35-39 for the other tested men. What does this tell us about where this change may have occurred?

The change could have occurred in Perry (21) or Robert (33). It cannot be narrowed any further by testing the men shown in the family chart.

f. When all of the differences are counted, there are three markers that vary between these men (DYS464, DYS449, and CDY). As stated earlier, a fourth difference is seen in DYS607 between these men and others who are in the same group in the Smith surname project. When four differences exist at 37 tested markers, test-takers are "distantly related," while three differences would indicate test-takers are "related." Are there other factors to incorporate in the analysis?

Yes. The three markers that vary between the five men shown in the table are all fast-moving markers. The fourth marker that differentiates them from other Smith men is shared by all of these suspected descendants of Henry (1). Strong documentary evidence links Henry (1) and Henry Jr. (5) and all descendants of that line. Strong documentary evidence links George (4) to Ira (43). When we map the Y-STR marker differences to the family chart, the DNA is consistent with George (4) being a son of Henry (1). The fact that there are more mutations than expected can be explained somewhat because of the prevalence of fast-moving markers.

g. Could additional DNA testing provide more evidence to apply to this research question?

Testing descendants of the other George Smith who lived in this area and finding that they have a different Y-DNA haplogroup would offer more supporting evidence. As we have already researched the people shown on this chart and many have already supplied a DNA sample, asking for atDNA tests may be easier and more productive in obtaining evidence to further support or contradict our hypothesis.

7. All of the living cousins (those listed last in each line on the chart) agree to take an atDNA test. The table below shows selected fields of the cousins' entries from the match list of Ira Smith (43).

Selected atDNA match list items for Ira Smith (43), accessed 21 July 2014			
Match	Total Shared DNA (cM)	Longest Segment (cM)	Predicted Relationship
Robert Smith (33)	115.51	25.49	2nd to 4th cousin
Tommy Curtis (41)	80.01	33.63	2nd to 4th cousin
Edward Walker (42)	38.50	11.58	4th to remote cousin
Louis Smith Jr. (44)	60.76	13.34	3rd to 5th cousin
Bobby Smith (45)	35.13	8.15	5th to remote cousin
Alfred Smith Jr. (46)	41.92	9.06	5th to remote cousin

a. Is this a reasonably sized group of test-takers to possibly lead to credible conclusions about relationships?

The seven test-takers in the table (Ira and six cousins named in his match list) form a reasonably large group of descendants from a common ancestor. The more DNA test-takers comprising a group, the less chance there is of an erroneous conclusion.

b. What might be a first step in analysis?

A first level of credibility in genetic-genealogy analysis is reached by verifying that all of these matches name Henry Smith (1) and his unknown spouse as common ancestors and that the matches share no other common ancestors. Because each of the cousins shares DNA with Ira (43), we know they are related to Ira. Because the only common ancestor in each cousin's tree is Henry (1), we theorize the shared atDNA was inherited from him.

c. Should we be concerned about the depth and accuracy of the test-takers' trees?

It is important to confirm that all of the test-takers have an accurate family tree with strong documentary evidence supporting the kinship conclusions. The trees should be deep enough to confirm these test-takers do not share a second set of common ancestors. If the trees are deep and accurate we can theorize that the atDNA confirms this ancestral link. However, this match list for Ira (43) confirms only his shared DNA with each of the others. The list does not indicate whether any of the matches share DNA with each other.

d. Using the information in the table, what might be a next step in our analysis?

A second level of credibility is obtained by confirming that the total amount of shared DNA and the longest segments shared are within the limits expected for the actual relationship shared by the test-takers. (When Family Tree DNA is the testing company, we generally remove segments smaller than 5 cM to obtain the total shared DNA of blocks 5 cM and larger in size.) This can be verified by accessing the statistics for atDNA in the ISOGG Wiki.[1] The Shared Centimorgan Project documents actual shared cM values seen in real-life situations.[2] Real-life numbers vary significantly from statistical averages. In this exercise, the total amounts of shared DNA and the longest shared blocks are within the limits expected based on the relationships between the test-takers as shown in the family tree.

The table below is a matrix indicating which cousins show as "In Common With" each other.

In Common With matrix for the Smith cousins (manually created to include all test-takers)							
	Ira (43)	Robert (33)	Tommy (41)	Edward (42)	Louis Jr. (44)	Bobby (45)	Alfred Jr. (46)
Ira (43)	SELF	Yes	Yes	Yes	Yes	Yes	Yes
Robert (33)	Yes	SELF	Yes	Yes	Yes	Yes	Yes
Tommy (41)	Yes	Yes	SELF	Yes	Yes	Yes	Yes
Edward (42)	Yes	Yes	Yes	SELF	Yes	Yes	Yes
Louis Jr. (44)	Yes	Yes	Yes	Yes	SELF	Yes	Yes
Bobby (45)	Yes	Yes	Yes	Yes	Yes	SELF	Yes
Alfred Jr. (46)	Yes	Yes	Yes	Yes	Yes	Yes	SELF

e. Using the information in the table, what might be a next step in our analysis?

The third level of credibility is obtained by confirming all or most of the test-takers also share DNA with each other. This can be done using the "In Common With" tool provided by some testing companies and third-party websites. The table above was manually created based on graphic displays from multiple runs of an "In Common With" tool on a testing-company site. The same list of names is on the top row and in the left column. Cells containing the word "SELF" indicate locations where the person named on the top row is the same person named in the left column. Cells containing "Yes" indicate the person named in the left column shares DNA with the person named at the top of the intersecting column. This indicates the two share DNA somewhere on the chromosomes, but not necessarily on the same segment as other matches listed. For example,

---

[1] "Autosomal DNA Statistics," *ISOGG Wiki* (http://isogg.org/wiki/Autosomal_DNA_statistics).

[2] Blaine Bettinger, "The Shared cM Project," *The Genetic Genealogist*, 29 May 2015 (http://thegeneticgenealogist.com/2015/05/29/the-shared-cm-project/).

Robert may share DNA with Ira and Tommy on chromosome 6, yet share DNA on chromosome 7 with other named test-takers.

The table below shows selected elements of the resulting segment analysis. Small segments and matches from others not shown in this family chart have been eliminated. The items grouped at the top of the table would be found while logged in to the account of Ira Smith (43); his name is in the left column. The items grouped at the bottom of the table would be found while logged in to the account of Edward Walker (42); his name is in the left column.

Shared segment details for selected segments for Ira Smith (43) and cousins, and for Edward Walker (42) and cousins							
Tested person	Match Name	Chr	Start	Stop	cM	SNPs	Rel
Ira (43)	Tommy (41)	6	135113519	160850541	33.63	7101	4C
Ira (43)	Robert (33)	6	134769313	151510948	19.33	4154	3C1R
Ira (43)	Edward (42)	6	151306471	158850732	11.58	2290	4C
Ira (43)	Robert (33)	7	27322710	47468816	25.49	5563	3C1R
Ira (43)	Edward (42)	7	27723126	34259818	8.72	1984	4C
Ira (43)	Louis Jr. (44)	7	27322710	36912091	13.34	2881	4C
Ira (43)	Bobby (45)	7	25785734	30894793	8.15	1583	4C
Ira (43)	Alfred Jr. (46)	7	25785734	31479397	9.06	1784	4C
Edward (42)	Ira (43)	6	151306471	158850732	11.58	2290	4C
Edward (42)	Tommy (41)	6	151306471	158850732	11.58	2290	3C
Edward (42)	Robert (33)	6	Note 1				3C1R
Edward (42)	Ira (43)	7	27723126	34259818	8.72	1984	4C
Edward (42)	Robert (33)	7	27723126	34259818	8.72	1984	3C1R
Edward (42)	Louis Jr. (44)	7	27723126	34259818	8.72	1984	4C
Edward (42)	Bobby (45)	7	Note 1				4C
Edward (42)	Alfred Jr. (46)	7	Note 1				4C
Note 1. No shared segment is shown, but the cousins' names are included here so the list is complete. The overlapping segment may have been among the small segments removed before beginning analysis. This can be confirmed by checking the detailed shared-segment data without removing the small segments.							

f. Using the information in the table above, what might be the next step in our analysis?

A fourth level of credibility is obtained by comparing shared DNA segments of a significant size (as defined in the atDNA chapter). Triangulating involves looking for DNA segments with the same or overlapping start and end points shared by multiple test-takers believed to be in the same family tree. Triangulation does not always work due to random recombination and inheritance. Triangulation requires an investment of time in analyzing the shared DNA segments.

On chromosome 6, Ira (43) shares a significant portion of an overlapping segment with Tommy (41), Robert (33), and Edward (42). Ira, Edward, and Tommy form a confirmed triangulated group on this DNA segment. Robert's segment shares a very small overlap (151306471–151510948) with the segment shared by Edward and Ira. Because of this Robert does not appear on Edward's segment-details list when we only include large segments. In some cases this might indicate Robert is related to Ira on a different line than is Edward and Tommy. Further analysis of the shared DNA segments may provide more evidence to determine whether this is the case.

On chromosome 7, Ira (43) shares an overlapping segment with Robert (33), Edward (42), Louis Jr. (44), Bobby (45), and Alfred Jr. (46). Edward shares that same overlapping segment with Ira, Robert, and Louis, but not Bobby and Alfred. While Edward may share a small portion of this segment with Bobby and Alfred, the shared amount was too small to be found in our list. However, the fact that Edward shares an overlapping segment on chromosome 7 with Ira, Robert, and Louis more likely indicates Edward and Robert are related through the same ancestral line as Ira, even though Robert did not inherit a large enough segment of chromosome 6 to figure into the analysis in the previous paragraph. A thoroughly researched and well-documented family tree that is deep enough to rule out another common ancestor adds more evidence in support of a conclusion these shared segments came from Henry Smith (1) or his mate.

The Y-STR and atDNA evidence together support the conclusions that George (4) is a son of Henry (1). If Tommy (41) also takes an mtDNA test we can answer a second question by confirming or refuting the family legend that Henry Smith (1) was married to a Choctaw woman who was the mother of his children.

Chapter 8 Exercise Answers

1. The following test-takers are identified as a match using the "One-to-One" tool at GEDmatch. Write a citation for this match.

> Test-taker 1: Kyle Lyons (GEDmatch kit A001234) (source: AncestryDNA)
> Test-taker 2: Ron Gough (GEDmatch kit M002345) (source: 23andMe)

> GEDmatch One-to-One matching segments (7 cM threshold):

Chromosome	Start	End	Centimorgans	SNPs
1	222,127,692	236,160,966	22.3	3,952
12	126,612,824	132,276,195	20.2	2,062

> Largest segment=22.3 cM
> Total of segments > 7 cM=42.5 cM
> Estimated number of generations to MRCA=4.4

> GEDmatch, "One-to-One DNA Comparison," database report, v2, *GEDmatch* (http://gedmatch.com/ : accessed 1 October 2014), Kyle Lyons, kit A001234; Ron Gough, kit M002345; 22.5 cM total, longest block 22.3 cM; 22.3 cM on chromosome 1 (start–stop points: 222127692–236160966); 20.2 cM on chromosome 12 (start–stop points: 126612824–132276195).

2. Using the tables in question 7 of the "Incorporating DNA Testing in a Family Study" chapter, write a citation for the segments shared by Ira Smith (43) and Robert Smith (33).

> "Family Finder," database report, *Family Tree DNA* (https://familytreedna.com/ : accessed 21 July 2014), for Ira Smith and Robert Smith, predicted 2nd to 4th cousins; matches on chromosome 6 (start–stop points: 134769313–151510948), 19.33 cM, and chromosome 7 (start–stop points: 27322710–47468816), 25.49 cM; documented relationship 3rd cousins once-removed.

3. Write a proof argument based on your own research or one of the exercises in this book. Use the *National Genealogical Society Quarterly* articles listed in this chapter as models. Form a study group with your peers, join a writing group, or ask a friend to critique your proof argument. After you feel comfortable with your writing, consider submitting the article for possible publication in a local, state, regional, or national journal, or enter a genealogical writing contest. Lists of writing competitions can be found online.[1]

---

[1] Powell, "Genealogical Competitions, Scholarships & Contests." Hait, "Genealogy Writing Competitions." Also see results from an Internet search for "genealogical writing contest.